THE PROFESSIONAL HOLIDAY HOME

BUYING, MANAGING AND ENJOYING YOUR
HOME AWAY FROM HOME — PROFITABLY

CRAIG REID

The Professional Holiday Home - Buying, Running & Enjoying Your Home Away From Home - Profitably

Copyright © Craig Reid 2021

www.professionalholidayhomes.com

The moral right of Craig Reid to be identified as the author of this work has been asserted in accordance with the Copyright Act 1968.

All rights reserved. No part of this publication may be reproduced or transmitted by any means, electronic, photocopying or otherwise without prior written permission of the author.

First published in Australia 2021 by Craig Reid.

ISBN 978-0-9945949-3-8

Disclaimer

All information contained within this book constitutes general advice only and is not in any way intended for any individual. Should the reader choose to make use of the information contained within, this is entirely their decision and the author, publisher and their representatives do not assume any responsibility whatsoever under any conditions or circumstances. Individuals should seek their own professional advice applicable to their specific situation. Any opinions expressed in this work are exclusively those of the author.

The Professional Holiday Home:

Buying, Managing and Enjoying
Your Home Away from Home — Profitably

Contents

About This Book 1

Part 1: Buying a Holiday Rental 3

    Introduction: Living the Dream 5
    Our Story 7
    The Holiday Rental Market 10
    What's Important to Guests When Booking? 11
    The Sharing Economy and Technology 13
    The Alternative to Hotels 13
    The Threat of Regulation 14
    Families and Pets 15
    Don't Be 'That House' 16
    Why Buy A Holiday Rental Property 18
    Assessing a Property to Buy 24
    Competition 30
    Calendar Data 31
    Pricing Comparisons 32
    Sleeping With the Enemy 33
    Committing to Buy 34
    When to Buy 35
    Checking Regulations and Laws 36

Part 2: Setting Up Your Holiday Rental Property 37

    Building 38
    Renovating 39
    Refreshing the Property 41
    Privacy 42
    Plumbing and Electricity 43
    Furnishing 44
    Living Areas 45
    What to Provide 45
    Dining Room 48
    Bedrooms 49
    Kitchen 49
    Bathrooms 55
    Laundry 56

Decks/Patios/Verandas 57
Keys/Keyless Entry 59
CCTV Cameras 60
Alarm Systems 61
Other Recommended Facilities 61
Pets 62
Linen 63
Fire Safety 65
Consumables/Pantry Items 65
Garbage Cans 68
Damage and Extra Fees 68
Staff 69
Insurance 76
Set-up Checklist 78

Part 3: Listing Your Property for Rental 84

Naming Your Property 85
Avoiding Common Mistakes 86
Listing Your Property Online 92
Photos 93
Floor Plans 99
Virtual Tours 99
Video 100
Property Description 101
Rules 105
Pricing 106
Analysing the Competition 109
Booking Window 114
Base Price 114
Bond (security deposit) 114
Minimum Stay Periods 115
Deposit 115
Documenting Your Pricing 116
Dynamic Pricing 117
Guest Guidebook 117
Frequently Asked Questions (FAQs) 119
Terms and Conditions 121
Cancellations 122
Websites to List on 122
Your Own Website – Is It Worth It? 130
Online Booking Systems 133
Channel Management Software 134
Payment Gateways 134
Managing Enquiries and Bookings 136
Responding to Guest Enquiries 137
Vetting Guests 137

- Declining Guests 141
- Following Up 142
- Booking and Payment 143
- Instant Bookings 143
- Guest Acceptance 144
- Payment Methods 144
- Updating Calendars 145
- Sending Guests Information 145
- Notifying Cleaners 146
- The Guest Stay 146
- Welcome Packs 148
- Visitor Book 149
- Guest Complaints 149
- Emergencies and Disasters 150
- Check-out 151
- Cleaning and Inspection 152
- Stocking Up 152
- Early Check-in/Late Check-out 153
- Bond Refunds and Extra Charges 154
- Guest Reviews 155

Marketing Your Property 157

Case Studies 163

About This Book

This book is designed to help you through all the stages of holiday rental ownership, from buying the right property, to setting up your property for rental then the process of managing your holiday rental to achieve success.

Technology is moving at such a fast pace that by the time you are reading this book the booking websites will have changed several times. To mitigate this, the focus of this book is on the key success factors that are applicable to any booking website irrespective of the changes that occur – rather than a deep dive into their functionality.

The book has been specifically written for a typical holiday rental owner. That person is busy with their career, lives a 2–3 hour drive from their property and therefore has only 1–2 hours a week to spend managing it.

Not only is the book a checklist of everything you need to do, but it also covers how to avoid the pitfalls and embrace the quick wins to build a holiday rental that is not only easy to run but which is profitable and professional.

PART 1:

Buying a Holiday Rental

Introduction: Living the Dream

Think back to that day you were on holiday. That day you were enjoying so much. Maybe you were splashing in the water at the beach or strolling through the countryside. It was a day you wished could last forever. Maybe you wandered through the town you were visiting and stopped to look in the real estate agents' windows ... and dreamed of what could be. Then you realised that maybe the dream wasn't so far out of reach – after all, that cosy cottage you were staying at was a holiday rental property too. Why couldn't you do the same thing?

There is no reason why you can't. Hundreds of thousands of others around the world have done so, and they enjoy their properties whilst also creating a fantastic income stream. You can do that too. Sadly, though, for some people, a holiday rental can become an albatross around their neck. Poor booking numbers, high maintenance costs or simply a lack of a customer base can lead to huge disappointment and financial problems. But that isn't going to be you!

As the CEO and founder of Professional Holiday Homes and the owner of two highly profitable, multi-award winning properties I will walk you through every step you need to successfully buy, run and enjoy your new home away from home. More importantly, I will show you proven methods for achieving maximum bookings with minimum effort.

Introduction: Living the Dream

Our Story

Like many others we fell in love with the sleepy seaside town of Callala Beach when we visited the Jervis Bay area on holiday. All the variables seemed right: under three hours from our home in Sydney (not too long a drive for a weekend), a beach as beautiful as a tropical island and an untouched charm that reminded us of the seaside holidays of our childhoods. In short, it was love at first sight.

We spent some time visiting Callala Beach and talking to a few real estate agents before deciding that we wanted to take the plunge and buy a property. As new parents of twin boys we felt it would be more convenient enjoying holidays close to home as opposed to getting on a plane with two babies. Making the decision was the easy part. Over the next two years we went through the Global Financial Crisis, stopped looking for a while then realising that the property market had plateaued, summoned up the courage to buy. We spent several months looking at different properties before we found one that had the right beach house charm. We bought it the day it came on the market and we settled on the property in April 2009. We called it Hayes Beach House after Hayes Cottage in the Shetland Islands in Scotland where my mother and grandmother were born.

There was a lot of work to be done and we found an excellent builder and renovated the property inside and out just in time for the busy summer season. In November 2009 we listed the property on a single website with minimal expectations as to how many bookings we would receive (after all, a local real estate agent had told us optimistically that we might get 4–6 weeks of rentals per year). Within the first few days we were inundated with enquiries for the Christmas and January holiday period.

Looking back we have to laugh at how we handled those first enquiries. We honestly thought that if someone sent in an enquiry it meant that they wanted to book. We spent about a day plotting a large number of enquiries against a calendar then sending out responses – fully expecting them to slot in neatly like a jigsaw puzzle. Of course, most of them decided not to book and we learned our first lesson: if they want to book, take the booking. The calendar will work itself out.

In that first year we were delighted simply to be paying our mortgage and we did that within our first six months of renting the property. We were bitten by the bug at that point and started to look at the many websites we could list the property on. We also put processes in place to streamline the amount of effort required to manage the enquiry and booking process. Over the next three years we experimented with listing on a range of websites – some good, some bad, some incredibly ugly (in terms of return on investment). We also started to enter the local tourism awards and were happy to be listed as a finalist in 2011. We started to build up a huge number of positive reviews and this was a big factor in us winning the Stayz.com.au award for best pet-friendly NSW in 2013. We then followed this by winning Silver at the South Coast Tourism Awards in 2014.

In 2016 we bought our second property Sunbaker Beach House at Culburra Beach, a 15-minute drive from our first property. It was summer and we got Sunbaker up for rental quickly. We didn't renovate but did a few touch ups to get it shipshape, added new furniture and had it on the market for the last two months of summer which brought in some much needed cash. In winter 2016 we renovated the property throughout.

We had expected Sunbaker to do well but didn't expect it would match Hayes in bookings in its first year – and that's exactly what it did. In fact it often exceeded Hayes' bookings for some months of the year. By the end of the financial year Sunbaker had achieved $81k in bookings. Not bad for a humble beach shack a four-minute walk from the beach!

It was at this point that we realised that we could achieve the same incredible results for other properties, and in mid-2017 our company, Professional Holiday Homes was born. We took on our first client in June 2017 and have grown steadily ever since. Our consistent track record of increasing our clients' bookings has given us a terrific reputation in the marketplace.

Hayes and Sunbaker continue to be two of the busiest properties in the Jervis Bay area and we still get to enjoy them too.

All of this success required experimentation and trial and error to get things right. The good news is that by reading this book you don't need to go through that!

The Holiday Rental Market

The holiday rental market is growing steadily globally but a few aspects may surprise you.

Firstly, awareness of the concept of holiday rentals is growing but is surprisingly still new to many guests. You may be amazed to hear that it is not uncommon in this day and age to have guests have their first ever stay at a holiday rental. These guests need extra guidance and reassurance.

Most guests still look to hotels as the first option when booking accommodation. But with websites that were traditionally focused on hotels welcoming holiday rentals, the lines between hotels and holiday rentals are blurring. Guests still feel that hotels are easier to book than holiday rentals and this will remain until there comes a time when all holiday rentals are instantly bookable like hotels.

But when guests do stay at a holiday rental for the first time, the experience is a powerfully positive one. Guests are not only highly satisfied but it's not unusual for them to become raving fans of the concept. In fact, satisfaction levels outstrip hotels by a considerable margin. As would be expected most guests eschew 'traditional' methods of booking such as phone calls and prefer to book online.

In terms of management of properties many owners choose to manage properties themselves but property managers are also a popular choice for those lacking time or the technical skills to manage what is effectively an online business.

What's Important to Guests When Booking?

Guest expectations are increasing year on year, but what are the factors that are most important to them when they look to book a property?

Here are the top 10 most important factors:

Ability to instant book

Guests want a 'hotel style' booking experience where their booking is confirmed and paid on the spot. They don't want to wait around for twenty-four hours to be told that their chosen property is unavailable and that their plans have been thrown into chaos!

Guest reviews

Guests want to read reviews before booking, and the more the better. Reviews are a powerful way of providing trust to the guest.

Up-to-date property information

If a property listing looks neglected or inaccurate it waves a red flag to the guest and the guest can rapidly lose confidence in their booking decision. Missing information indicates to the guest that the overall service may be below par.

Location (map)

Guests are not happy just to know what area the property is in; they want to know the exact location right down to the street number. Distance to key attractions such as beaches and tourist attractions are critical and guests want to be able to identify how far they are right down to how many minutes walk. They want to see exactly where the home is on the map.

Photos

Quality and quantity are both critical when it comes to photos. Amateurish, dark or fuzzy photos send a message to the guest that the rest of their experience will be amateurish too. Guests expect to see high quality photos of every part of the property and surrounds.

Rates

Guests expect that the rate they see is the rate they pay. Adding on undisclosed fees is a sure-fire way to upset a guest and gain a negative review.

Payment options

Accepting all major credit and debit cards online is now the norm. Guests are also now looking to use online payment systems such as Paypal. Asking guests to pay by bank deposits, cheques or obscure payment platforms should be avoided at all costs.

Amenities

Along with accurate descriptions, it is critically important that the correct amenities are selected on the booking websites (typically these will be tick box options). The reason that these are so important is that guests can often filter search results based on amenities – and if an amenity hasn't been selected the property won't be displayed in search results.

Property description

The property description is often what separates the wheat from the chaff. Having a well-crafted description elevates a property above the others. Often the property description is used as a long list of property amenities when it is best placed to set the scene through an experiential description where the guest can already see themselves enjoying the property.

Response time

Where properties don't have Instant Booking the time taken for an owner to accept a booking is critical. If owners aren't accepting bookings in under 30 minutes they simply aren't competing. Guests don't want to wait, which is why Instant Booking is now so critical to success.

The Sharing Economy and Technology

Holiday rentals have undergone a revolution in the last ten years primarily due to the technology available. Booking systems that were previously only the domain of hotels are now available to holiday rental owners on a global scale. Furthermore, this technology is powering the rise of the sharing economy ...

The sharing economy refers to the supply of excess capacity of a product or service and it is this premise that has led holiday rental owners to share their properties in return for income.

Whilst technology has improved dramatically, many holiday rentals are still not competing on a level playing field with hotels where immediate online booking is the norm. Whilst all of the major holiday rental websites now provide Instant Booking, a large proportion of holiday rental owners are still reluctant to use this functionality as they prefer to screen guests prior to accepting bookings. We'll discuss the importance of Instant Booking later.

The Alternative to Hotels

It's important to recognise that rather than being a direct competitor to hotels, holiday rentals can represent an alternative. For small groups or single business travellers hotels may often be a more suitable option – and of course there are always guests who prefer the facilities of resorts such as multiple restaurants and waiters to bring cocktails to them by the pool! Smaller towns in regional areas may not even have a hotel – so holiday rentals have opened up these areas to a whole new tourism market.

Where holiday rentals come into their own is when a family or a group wishes to find accommodation. Larger groups (greater than 4 guests) staying at hotels are often forced to hire multiple rooms or expensive suites. Holiday rentals typically provide greater space and multiple bedrooms which significantly reduce the cost per person.

Hotels are also struggling to keep pace with facilities provided in holiday rentals and customers are becoming increasingly disillusioned with the experience. Holiday rentals can provide a self-contained accommodation experience where guests don't have to share facilities with others. They don't need to dine in overpriced restaurants or pay through the nose for in-house movies. They can cook on a BBQ in the fresh air or enjoy Netflix – all included in the price.

A guest says ...

At a 5-star hotel resort, our family of six were forced to pay for two interconnecting rooms. As a mother this worried me as the kids had to sleep in another room. The resort's draconian rules meant that we were not allowed to stay in a family villa, even though we could easily have fitted in it. Whilst the resort was of a high standard the cost was also very high and we were forced to eat in the same restaurants over the period of two weeks as there were no cooking facilities within the rooms. The kids were bored in the evenings and the in-house movies cost $12 each! There was no stereo in the room to play music and the TV was outdated. We could have hired a lovely holiday rental for a fraction of the price.

The Threat of Regulation

The rise in popularity of Airbnb was both a blessing and a curse for the holiday rental industry. On one hand Airbnb raised the profile and popularity of holiday rentals whilst on the other highlighted a number of issues which have tarnished the industry.

Firstly a minority of owners who ran their properties unprofessionally have been responsible for disturbances to neighbours. Stories of party houses are gleefully grabbed by the media and used to promote the false argument that holiday rentals are a significant cause of disturbance to local communities. Residents of apartment blocks have been particularly vocal in their opposition.

Much of the criticism has come as a result of short-term rentals in cities rather than in regional areas. The reality is that holiday rentals provide greater tourist numbers that bring much needed income to regional towns and communities that rely on tourism to survive. Many of these towns do not have hotels or motels and therefore holiday rentals provide a vital source of tourism.

The second factor that is again focused on city short-term rentals relates to the availability and affordability of housing. Short-term rentals have been criticised as reducing housing stock and thereby driving up prices.

There is certainly some truth to these claims, but it is also evident that the hotel industry is continually engaging in dirty tricks to try to mitigate the growing threat of holiday rentals on their market share. A common strategy of the hotel industry is to write articles for popular publications highlighting only the negative aspects of holiday rentals.

Third, the industry has been criticised for a lack of standards, particularly around guest safety. Again the hotel industry has been vocal in this criticism, citing that they have to meet regulations that holiday rentals do not. There is some merit in these criticisms given that some holiday rentals lack basic fire and safety facilities and adequate insurance to protect owners and guests.

It is a reality of the industry that if regulations are not currently in place in your area you can expect them to come soon.

Families and Pets

Often holiday rentals represent better value and have significantly better space and amenities, particularly for families.

Whilst kids may love the hotel pool there is no need to worry about annoying other guests at a holiday rental. Another area where hotels can't compete is in pet-friendly accommodation. Pets (particularly dogs) are considered a part of the family and leaving them at home is a stressful and expensive experience for many dog owners. Being able to bring 4-legged friends with them is great for the guest experience particularly when visiting country locations or the beach. Off-leash areas where dogs can exercise and play are becoming increasingly common. Switched-on holiday rental owners are actively marketing their properties as pet friendly and offering facilities for dogs such as kennels, bedding and dog toys.

Recent research by HomeAway has shown that 30% of guests are looking for pet-friendly accommodation so if your holiday rental doesn't cater for pets you are missing a significant slice of the potential market.

Don't Be 'That House'

Sadly there are some holiday rental owners that are spoiling the reputation of the industry through their ownership of so-called 'party houses'. These operators show disregard for neighbours and allow their properties to be occupied by large groups of guests who often become drunk, noisy and generally unruly. These properties become the target of irate neighbours and the local press who take great pleasure in publicising them.

Thankfully these party houses are few and far between with the vast majority of holiday rental owners not willing to entertain such guests. Unfortunately, media attention on a few of these properties is continuing to tarnish the reputation of the holiday rental industry.

The other focus of media attention is the instance of guests trashing holiday rentals. Again these cases are often blown out of proportion by the media and the risk of it occurring is lowered considerably when professionally managed.

Why Buy a Holiday Rental Property?

Buying property for investment purposes is popular the world over. But most investors choose the option of long-term leasing rentals rather than go down the path of owning a holiday rental property. Often they feel afraid to buy in an area that isn't close to home and which they don't know well. On the flip side they can have a property that they can enjoy for holidays and make great returns. Let's look at the pros and cons in more detail ...

Pros

Saving Money on Holidays

Holiday rental owners can save thousands of dollars per year by using their own homes for weekends away as well as longer breaks. There is no need to pay for expensive flights if the home is within driving distance (particularly convenient if you have a young family or a dog). Other than petrol costs and maybe a post-stay clean (if you don't want to clean it yourself), there are few costs involved assuming your rental income is covering your costs.

Getting Away More Often

Having a holiday rental a few hours drive away means that you can hop in the car and enjoy a weekend away at the drop of a hat. What would ordinarily cost a great deal of money to rent can now be enjoyed for free (presuming your rental income covers your home loan repayments). Naturally some holiday rental owners choose to buy properties far from home, but these are in the minority.

Investment (capital gains)

Holiday rentals can be as good an investment in terms of capital gains as any other property. A carefully selected holiday rental in the correct location can bring substantial gains over time.

An owner says ...

We bought our first holiday rental for $316k. Including renovations we spent approximately $350k. It is now worth $700k – a $350k gain in nine years.

Bear in mind that due to capital gains your property is likely to be subject to additional taxes when you sell it. Check with your accountant for further details.

Income

The biggest pro with a holiday rental is arguably the amount of rental income that can be generated. If the property is run and marketed effectively the rental returns can be significantly higher than a long-term lease (and you get to enjoy it yourself too!)

An owner says ...

On the long-term property leasing market our property would rent for $300 a week. Our rental income running it as a holiday rental is more than five times that amount!

Share with Others

Not only does your level of coolness increase exponentially when you tell family and friends that you have a holiday rental, it's also great to be able to share your home with them. You'll also be surprised at how many of them are happy to pay to stay there (with a little friends' discount of course!)

An owner says ...

You are not a charity – don't go giving up your income so friends can stay for free. You are running a business. Decide what percentage to offer your friends and family and stick to it. You will find that most are freeloaders who will not ask again when they find out they have to pay.

Charity

Having a holiday rental also helps you do something great for the world. The majority of holiday rentals have spare capacity at some stage during the year, and a great thing to do is to donate any spare capacity you may have to a charity to provide free accommodation for those in need.

An owner says ...

At our holiday rental we have some capacity over the colder winter months so we donate this capacity to a charity that helps women with breast cancer so that they can stay at the property for free.

Cons

Groundhog Day (same place each time)

If you buy a holiday rental you'd better make sure that you love the house and the area that it's in as you'll be spending a lot of time there. If you don't have a passion for it or you are someone who craves constant variety of locations, a holiday rental may not be right for you.

An owner says ...

We have owned our holiday rental for six years and we've never lost the love for the house or location. In fact, as time has gone by we've become increasingly more attached to it as we make many lifelong family memories of our time spent there.

Expense of Borrowing

Unless you're significantly financially endowed it's likely that you may need to borrow money to buy your property. The amount you need to borrow needs to be carefully weighed up against the potential rental income or you could find yourself in financial difficulties. It's also important to remember that holiday rentals can be highly seasonal and revenue may peak in particular times of the year and be non-existent in others. However, you still have to pay for loans every month so it's important to plan for the peaks and troughs of income.

An owner says ...

Our holiday rental is located at the beach and as a result we make 70% of our income in the summer months. In the early days we had to be careful to set aside some of the summer income to cover home loan payments in the quieter winter months.

Expense of Setting Up

In contrast to long-term leasing properties which may not require furnishing, holiday rental properties require a significant upfront investment in furnishing to ensure that an acceptable standard is created for guests (and the larger the property, the larger the expense).

Time Taken to Manage the Property

Some owners can find managing their properties time consuming and stressful, particularly if they are not Internet savvy or experienced in running a business. Finding staff to clean and maintain the property can also be difficult in some areas, particularly if the property is remote.

An owner says ...

Whilst we enjoy owning a holiday rental and we earn good money from it we found that we just weren't good at marketing or managing the property. We were happy to spend a bit more money to have an agency manage it for us. Many people like to do it themselves but for our personal situation that was the right decision for us.

Use It and Lose It

The irony of owning a holiday rental is that often when you want to use it most, so does everyone else. If you use the property in peak periods you may live with the *buyers' remorse* of lost income. Or in the opposite situation, if you don't use the property when you really want to you may feel that buying it has not been worthwhile.

An owner says ...

Our property has become so busy that we now have to book dates for ourselves. We've come to terms with the fact that we'd rather have the income from peak season than spend the time there ourselves. We've found a balance by staying for a couple of days a month in peak season and enjoying more time at the house during off-peak periods.

Assessing a Property to Buy

Purchasing a holiday rental is a very different experience to purchasing a residential property for yourself. Not only do you have to decide if the house meets your own personal needs, but you also have to consider a range of factors that influence how it will operate as a business. Let's look at some of the key factors to consider.

Location: Distance from Major Cities

Distance is an important factor. If the property is within a 3-hour drive of a major city you stand a much better chance of attracting weekend guests, as anything further away starts to lose its appeal due to the time and distance involved. Outside of three hours, guests are unlikely to consider the location for weekend stays and you may be restricted to bookings predominantly during holiday periods or long weekends. Of course, it's also important to choose a destination that's easy for *you* to get to.

Another important factor is whether there is likely to be weekend or weekday custom (or both). Obviously if you are within an area that can attract both types of guests you are giving yourself an increased chance of success. However, there are still many profitable holiday rentals that are long distances from major population centres but these tend to gain bookings during longer holiday periods where owners will be happy to travel a full day to get there and will consequently stay for a longer period.

Local Attractions

Wherever your holiday rental is located it needs to have local attractions that will pull in guests. Let's look at some of the most popular attractions that act as a drawcard to attract guests.

Beaches

Beaches are an ever popular attraction for guests, and often guest numbers will peak significantly during the summer months. Guests love rustic beach shacks that remind them of their childhoods. Some guests look for busy beach locations to have a good time and enjoy nightlife whilst others seek the tranquillity of an untouched paradise.

When buying at a beach location carefully consider both the style of the house and the distance to the beach. It's important to have a style that appeals to guests – whether that's a rustic beach shack or a modern beach house. This creates a feeling of escape, rather than staying at a property which is like their own home. Guests seek to enjoy the warm weather and the sea so properties that have alfresco areas and are within a 5-minute walk to the beach can command premium rates.

Mountains

Mountains attract hillwalkers, mountaineers and skiers. Cabins, chalets and lodges provide the ambiance that guests are looking for. Mountains can be popular destinations in both summer and winter, but ski seasons attract premium prices.

When buying in a mountain location look for wood cabins, roaring log fires and proximity to ski fields as key variables. Mountain views and luxury features such as spa baths complete the premium picture.

Countryside

Farms, cottages and rustic buildings appeal to guests seeking the quiet solitude of the countryside. Guests come to these locations to escape from cities and to get back in touch with the simple life. Ever popular are areas with strong food and wine cultures. These areas are also capitalising on the available space they have by doubling as concert venues.

When buying in country locations it's important to balance the wildness of the country with an acceptable level of comfort.

A guest says ...

We once stayed at a holiday rental next to a lake within a forest. Whilst the location was lovely, when night fell we were attacked by mosquitos and were kept awake by a thousand frogs! All I wanted was a relaxing weekend and a bubble bath and had to shower in water that smelled like a swamp. We couldn't leave fast enough!

Historical Significance

History buffs will seek out areas of cultural significance. They will often take part in tours and will look for properties that reflect the history of the area they are visiting. Historical drawcards don't need to be ancient either – even one or two hundred years of history can bring in the tourists.

Cities

Those wishing to travel the world will often enjoy the convenience of flying into a major city and exploring locally. One of the key reasons for Airbnb's success is its abundance and range of accommodation in major cities throughout the world.

Guests visiting cities will also enjoy staying at a property that reflects the style of the area where they can live like a local. The most important factor for these properties is the proximity to the city's main tourist attractions, shopping, restaurants and cafes.

Buying in the Wrong Location

Sometimes owners have an 'if we build it they will come' approach to holiday rental properties. That is, they buy a property in a remote location with no tourism draw card. They think that because the property is an attractive or special property that guests will come there just for the property itself. The reality is that most guests come to stay at holiday rentals because they want to visit a particular area or attraction, rather than the home being the central reason for their stay. Of course there are 'destination properties' which are exceptions to this, but those kind of homes (think multi-million dollar houses or castles!) represent a tiny minority of holiday rentals. Unless the property is located in a holiday hotspot where guests tend to stay for a week or more and where guests are willing to fly or drive long distances, the majority of holiday rentals are best located within a 3-hour drive of a major city. Above three hours, guests will think twice about driving there for a weekend.

A guest says ...

Because most properties have a 2-night minimum stay, to go away for a weekend means that we have to stay on a Friday and Saturday night and return on the Sunday. As we are at work until 5pm we can't leave until about 6pm on the Friday night. This means that we are restricted to properties within a 3-hour drive otherwise it is too exhausting to drive late into the night, particularly with a car full of tired kids.

Size

A critical factor in buying a holiday rental is the size of the property, as this will directly impact the number of guests you can accommodate and consequently the price you can charge. In this section we'll look at how the size of the property influences the kind of guests you'll be able to accommodate.

It can be tempting to squeeze in as many guests as possible in order to raise the price you can charge, but this can make guests uncomfortable if the living, dining and entertaining areas are too small for the number of people. When setting capacity think about whether your guests can all sit comfortably in these areas together. When a property has a capacity greater than 10 guests it's advisable to have multiple living areas where guests can separate into two groups; e.g. adults and kids.

The more guests that you have the greater the wear and tear on the property will be – but you will find that the extra capacity will more than pay for this.

Small (1 Bedroom)

Single bedroom properties such as apartments or cabins are suitable for single guests or couples who wish to have catering facilities. If you are a young couple, spare a thought for the future when there may be more than two of you! Unless in a premium location and well-appointed the income from smaller properties can be somewhat limited. These properties also face significant competition from hotels and serviced apartments.

Not having a kitchen doesn't mean that you can't rent the property as a short-term rental. If priced accordingly even single rooms with a bathroom and no cooking facilities can be popular if in a good location.

Medium (2–3 Bedrooms)

With 2–3 bedroom holiday rentals, you have the ability to accommodate between 4–8 guests. With two bedrooms you can choose to create several different combinations depending upon the type of customers you want to target. For example:

2 Bedroom

Two queen beds to attract two couples that want to holiday together (four guests)

One queen bed and two single beds to attract a small family

One queen bed and four bunk beds to attract larger families

Two tri-bunks to cater for two couples or a couple with four children

3 Bedroom

Two queen beds and four bunk beds/tri-bunk to attract two families

Three queen beds to attract groups of couples

Large (4+ Bedrooms)

Three queen beds and four bunk beds/tri-bunk to attract multiple families and grandparents

Four queen beds to attract groups of couples

If in doubt, going for the largest capacity you can is often the best option. The more guests you can fit in the more you divide the cost by those that are paying and the property becomes more economical. For example, if a property sleeps eight and costs $1,000 a night for two families then the cost for each family is $500. If three families stay at a property that sleeps twelve at $1,200 a night, the cost is $400 per family.

An owner says ...

Don't forget the power of a good quality sofa bed! For those guests that are happy to squash in for a day or two, a sofa bed may just give them the extra room that they need at the price they want to pay. The sofa bed is our holiday rental's secret weapon!

Competition

Number of Competitors

The great thing about today's Internet age is that there is an abundance of information available online to help you assess your competitors and the demand for holiday rental accommodation.

Firstly, all holiday rental booking websites allow you to search for properties based on geographic area. Some will show you a map so that you can assess the importance of specific locations upon bookings.

You will be able to assess the number of properties in the area to identify how many competitors you are up against. Don't panic if there are a large number of competitors – this is also indicative of a healthy level of demand for holiday rentals. The challenge is for your property to offer something better or unique to be able to differentiate your home from the others currently available.

By scanning through properties on the booking websites you will notice that many will have poor quality amateur photos, uninspiring descriptions and unsophisticated pricing.

An owner says ...

Even though there were more than two hundred holiday rentals in the town we were looking to buy in, we were not overly concerned with the competition. We had assessed a broad range of them and found the majority of them to be poorly maintained, badly furnished and insufficiently marketed. We felt there was a huge opportunity to capture the market – and we were right!

Calendar Data

As well as details of the number of competing holiday rentals in an area, all of their booking data is available online too.

Unfortunately, historical data is not available, but by selecting a cross-section of different properties in the area you can build up a picture of the level of demand by looking at each of their calendars.

Bear in mind that whilst guests will book well in advance for peak periods, cheaper properties tend to fill up more rapidly. Premium priced properties, on average, will tend to book out closer to peak periods. Guests also frequently book last minute so looking months ahead at calendars may not provide an accurate reflection of the level of demand. Looking at calendar bookings for each property within the next 1–2 months will give a more accurate impression of demand. Bear in mind that due to seasonality bookings may vary considerably. Rather than having to wait 12 months to obtain the data to analyse the property before purchasing, a quicker way to analyse the market is to start your analysis at the beginning of peak periods. You may find that income from these peak periods is enough to provide comfort that your holiday rental is financially sustainable.

Be aware that there is a common practice amongst rental agencies that manage multiple properties where (against the rules of many websites) they do not block out dates in calendars. The reason they do this is to encourage enquiries for unavailable properties so that they can then attempt to push the guest into another available property. This is very frustrating for the customer and many consider it to be an unethical way of doing business. Try to avoid these properties when doing your analysis.

Also bear in mind that viewing the pricing of vacant properties can skew your perspective on the right price to charge. If a property is consistently empty it is likely that it is overpriced (presuming there is adequate demand in the area and that other local properties are busy). Ideally look for busy properties (calendars 70% or more full within the next month) that have a couple of gaps in their calendars – then identify the prices they are charging for those gaps.

Beware of properties that appear to be fully booked. They may have blocked out dates for their own personal use or they may be significantly underpriced. A tell-tale sign of this is that they are booked solid for months ahead. Of course they could also have a superstar listing – and this will be apparent from the quality of the listing *and* the property itself (but these kinds of listings are few and far between).

Pricing Comparisons

The other key data available online is pricing data. Good operators will have up-to-date pricing customised for different seasons and special events throughout the year. This can give you a good indication of what you can set your prices at. Take an average of your estimated nightly pricing and multiply it by your estimated nights per year (that you've obtained from competitors' calendar data) and you should have a rough estimate of potential turnover.

There are also websites such as AirDNA, Pricelabs and Beyond Pricing that can provide information on pricing and demand in specific areas.

Sleeping With the Enemy

When you have decided where you'll be buying your holiday rental you'll likely be travelling to visit the location several times to look at properties for sale. This is an ideal opportunity to check out your competition by staying at their properties. Be sure to stay at two to three of the most popular (and highest rated) properties you can find. *There is very little to be learned from poor quality operators.*

Take note of their performance at every stage of your experience: from booking right through to after your visit. Here are some of the key factors to assess:

1. Was their online listing easy to find?
2. Were they listed on multiple booking websites?
3. Did they have their own website with direct booking facility?
4. Were the property description and photos of good quality?
5. Were they fast to respond to your enquiry?
6. Was their calendar up-to-date?
7. Was the price as advertised?
8. Was the booking/payment process easy?
9. Did they provide convenient payment options?
10. Did they send you good quality information immediately post-payment?
11. Were you able to get to the property easily?
12. Was the information regarding its location accurate?
13. Was the property and its facilities as you expected?
14. Was the property clean and well maintained?
15. Were the beds comfortable?

16. Were there adequate instructions for all the facilities?
17. Were there clear rules/guidelines provided as to your stay and departure?
18. Did they send you a survey after your stay?
19. Did they provide an incentive to return?

An owner says ...

Be sure to take photos of properties you stay at so you can remember the good and bad aspects when you return home.

Committing to Buy

When you have made the decision to buy there are a few factors to consider ...

How Much to Spend

Whilst your own financial situation will determine how much you can afford to spend on the property it's a good idea to estimate how much income you'll need from rentals in order to cover your costs.

You can get a good idea of demand from assessing other properties' booking calendars and as a rough guide you can estimate income based on the number of weeks rental per year.

Here's an example of a basic estimate:

Number of Rental Weeks Per Year	15
Average Rental Per Week	$ 2,500
Estimated booking income	**$ 37,500**
Loan Repayments	$ 15,000
Cleaning	$ 4,500
Rates	$ 3,000
Utilities	$ 3,000
Maintenance/repairs	$ 2,000
Total Costs	$ 27,500
Profit/Loss	**$ 10,000**

Think carefully about what you want to achieve. Whilst some owners are happy to cover their costs and enjoy the property themselves, others want to make substantial profits. It's important that you do not stretch yourself financially – you do not want to feel like your holiday rental is a millstone around your neck.

An owner says ...

Don't forget that buying the property is just the start of your expenses. Make sure you budget for renovations and furnishing before you buy.

When to Buy

You are likely to find a lack of supply during peak periods due to the income available during these periods. You may find the best time to go shopping is in the low season when holiday rental owners may be looking to sell. Saying that, it is more than likely that you will not find many holiday rentals up for sale. Most holiday rentals (even when run poorly) still create a greater income for owners than long-term leasing and this makes many owners reluctant to sell.

You may also find that vendors selling current holiday rentals that are performing well may charge a premium due to the established rental income – similar to a business that has goodwill.

Checking Regulations and Laws

Before you make the decision to buy it's vitally important to check the regulations in the local area as well as the laws in your country to ensure that short-term rentals are permitted. Whilst some government authorities are supportive of holiday rentals as an important source of revenue, many holiday rental owners are increasingly finding themselves in hot water with local councils and government authorities for setting up holiday rentals and then finding out that they have breached rules and regulations. It is essential to check the laws in your area to understand if short-term rentals are permitted. Even if they are permitted there may be certain restrictions in place (for example a cap on the number of nights the property can be rented).

It's also very important to understand the rules that are applicable in your country regarding taxation, depreciation and capital gains. Advice from both a solicitor and accountant is recommended.

PART 2:
Setting Up Your Holiday Rental Property

As soon as you've signed on the dotted line to purchase the property, there's no time to waste! If the property is in a rentable condition then obtain copies of the photos that the real estate agent has used in the listing and list the property. Be sure to add a note to your listings indicating that you'll be improving the furniture in the photos. Guests will have no problem with the furniture being different to the photos as long as it's of better quality. Be sure to give yourself adequate time to finalise the sale and furnish the property by blocking out your booking calendars.

If the property isn't in a rentable condition and needs to be renovated, get that underway as quickly as you can and delay listing on rental websites until you have a better understanding of completion dates – renovations have a nasty habit of going on longer than you'd expect!

An owner says ...

Before we even owned the property we had $4,000 in advance bookings. We used the real estate agent's photos and added a comment in the listing saying that we'd be upgrading the furniture. You may have to price the property a little lower initially to get traction on bookings.

Let's look at what you need to do before listing it for rental for the first time.

Building

Rather than buying an existing property you may have decided to buy a patch of land and build a new house. This can be a good option in some areas but naturally will increase the time required before listing your property. With new build properties it's important to match the style of the property with the surrounding area. Think cosy cabin in the mountains or surf shack at the beach.

Renovating

Many holiday rental owners choose to renovate in order to put their stamp on a property that may be run down. This allows them to match the design with the surrounding area as well as to be able to raise the level of quality (and therefore the achievable level of revenue).

If you have easy access to tradespeople or are handy with a few tools renovating can be an attractive option – but remember that time spent renovating is time lost renting. Think about whether hiring a builder for a month is better than spending every one of your weekends for six months renovating (and thereby losing six months of income). Chances are you'd be better spending the money upfront, saving yourself a lot of stress and being able to enjoy your home instead of working on it.

Bear in mind that if you are renovating a property a long distance from home that this brings its own set of challenges. Before you start, stress to your tradespersons that you'll require regular updates (emails, texts and photos) to be sent showing progress. Be clear on your dates for when work needs to be completed.

Renovations are best scheduled in low season so that you can minimise revenue being lost. If you have acquired your property immediately prior to high season it may be worth furnishing the house, renting it through peak season and then renovating in low season so as it maximise revenue. You can then redirect the extra funds from peak season towards your renovations.

An owner says ...

We chose to buy a run-down shack. Whilst it had 'good bones' the property needed full renovation to realise its potential. Over a period of six months during low season our builder completed the renovations and we furnished the property. The end result was nothing short of spectacular and we could never have achieved the high levels of revenue we now receive if we had not renovated it. We finished the property just in time to list it at peak season and the money rolled in straight away.

Prioritising Renovations

Before commencing your renovations it's a good idea to create a list and prioritise the renovations based on what type of customers you want to attract. If you don't have enough money to do everything you want to immediately, take into account the climate, location and type of guests when setting your renovation priorities.

For example:

- Consider focusing on alfresco areas such as verandas and decks if in a warm climate; e.g. at the beach
- If in a cold climate such as a ski area consider investing in log fires, heating and a well-equipped laundry (for drying wet ski gear)
- Invest in secure fencing and gates if catering to dog owners
- For family-friendly properties consider kids play equipment or a cubby house
- For inner city apartments near the CBD, invest in a desk and comfortable office chair for business travellers.

It's also good to think about the type of groups you'll attract:

For example, if you have a ski lodge that caters for 25–30 year olds, focus on setting up for a combination of couples and singles.

If you have a beach house that sleeps 12, set it up to cater for three families with kids and dogs.

An owner says ...

In retrospect we should first have invested money in making our property dog-friendly by installing secure fencing. It wasn't until after we installed the fencing that we realised how large the pet-friendly market was in our area. It pays to research the market to understand what kind of guests you will be catering for.

A guest says ...

We stayed at a house near the snowfields. It was a nice property at first glance but it only had one gas fire and no clothes dryer. Every night we had to dry ski gear on chairs in front of the fire. As a family this meant that we had a lot of extra work as we had to dry the kids' ski gear. We couldn't believe they hadn't thought of it.

Refreshing the Property

Whether you have to do significant renovations or not it is always a good idea to give the property a refreshing lick of paint and a good scrub from top to bottom prior to furnishing. It can be very difficult to schedule painting and decorating within a busy booking schedule, so best to get it done before listing for rent.

An owner says ...

Little niggling problems can easily snowball so sort them out before you list. We had a door lock that was a little bit sticky. Fixing it prior to rental would have been preferable to receiving a call from a guest who had broken the key in the lock trying to get in. We had to change the lock including removing the door!

Privacy

No matter what type of property you have you must ensure that guests have privacy whether inside the property or in garden areas. Here are some areas to pay particular attention to.

If there are neighbouring properties ensure there is adequate fencing. Guests hate unfenced properties, particularly if they have pets.

If fencing isn't adequate to block neighbours from peering in, look at planting fast growing trees or shrubs to obscure views.

If the property is attached to another residence, ensure that the entrance is completely separate and that the other property cannot see into the holiday rental. Also take steps to ensure that adequate soundproofing is in place.

Be sure to be honest in your listing description if the property is attached to another residence. No matter how private it may be, some guests will always want a separate residence and will leave negative reviews if they feel the description has not been accurate.

An owner says ...

We own a 1-bedroom cottage attached to our own residence, but we've made it feel extremely private by installing soundproof walls, screening off the deck and having a dedicated private entrance.

Plumbing and Electricity

Guests on holiday aren't counting the cost of water or electricity used, so you will find that usage is typically higher than you will be paying at home. Also bear in mind that you may have guests that shower before they leave and guests that shower when they arrive – therefore potentially doubling the amount of people showering in one day. Be sure to check that your hot water system can cope with more than your maximum guest capacity and have your hot water system serviced regularly. As a rough guide, 40 Litres per guest is more than adequate.

An owner says ...

A guest turned up to find a flood at our property – the hot water system had exploded! We had to get an emergency plumber out which cost us $2,500 in addition to refunding the guest's booking. We immediately regretted not having it checked regularly. Thankfully we had loss of rent insurance that compensated us.

Most domestic hot water systems have a stated life of 10 years, but will almost always go for 15 years. Look to replace the system every 12.5 years during an off-season week rather than risk an emergency call-out at exorbitant rates.

Lighting

Be sure to replace any existing conventional light globes with LED light globes. Not only will they save you a lot of money they typically last for 10 years so you won't have guests complaining about blown light globes. Always have a good supply of spares for non-LED light globes.

A guest says ...

We turned up at a holiday rental to find almost every light globe in the bedrooms blown. We had to call the property manager to come out and replace them. Trying to get little kids to sleep in the dark in a strange house was not a great experience.

Furnishing

Outside of renovating a property, furnishing a holiday rental is likely to be your largest expense.

Make sure that you keep receipts of every item that you purchase for the house – whether a one-off expense (such as furniture) or an on-going expense (such as tea bags). Depending upon your country's tax laws these purchases may be tax deductible or depreciable.

The following sections detail the furnishings you'll need to help your property stand out from the crowd. Whilst secondhand furniture can sometimes work to create a particular style, be careful not to buy anything that looks worn or poorly maintained.

If you are in a rush to get your holiday rental on the market it may well be worth it to pay for some help to get furniture assembled. A lot of furniture these days is flat packed and can be time consuming to assemble.

An owner says ...

I spent several weekends over a number of months assembling furniture at my holiday rental, a few hours drive away. It took forever and I got more than my fair share of blisters! When I bought my next holiday rental I couldn't face doing the same thing again so I hired a handyman to put it together for me. It meant I got my property on the market much quicker and the rental revenue more than paid for the furniture assembly.

What to Provide

The following sections provide guidance on the set-up of your property based on successful, award-winning properties. If you follow these recommendations they will maximise the booking potential of your property. There are also some important safety guidelines that you should implement.

If you do not have time to implement these yourself, consider using a local tradesperson to do them for you.

Living Areas

Couch(es)

When buying a couch consider the capacity of your property and try to have enough seating for everyone. This doesn't mean you have to have a couch that seats your maximum capacity, but have a range of seating options for everyone – even if that means bean bags on the floor for kids.

If you can afford it, leather couches are a good option as they are easy to clean. Guests on holiday love to indulge and that means chocolatey fingers and the odd splash of wine on a couch. If you have a fabric couch, have fabric protection applied to make cleaning of stains easier.

Chairs

Having an easy chair or lounge chair can provide a nice place for guests to relax or read a book. Again leather is a good option.

TV/Netflix

You should have a large, high definition smart TV at the property with Netflix (you will require Wi-Fi to have Netflix). If purchasing a new TV check with the retailer that the TV has the Netflix app as not all brands have this. Many guests prefer the convenience of Netflix to cable/satellite. You should pay for the Netflix account rather than expecting guests to log into their own Netflix account. Not everyone has a Netflix account at home.

A guest says ...

We stayed at a multi-million dollar waterfront property. We couldn't believe it when we tried to access Netflix that the owner hadn't paid for an account. It seemed stingy and left a bad taste in my mouth.

DVD

If you have access to Netflix (or another good streaming service) you don't need to worry about having a DVD Player and DVDs. However, if you are in a remote area that doesn't have good Internet access, a DVD player can be a good option.

If you do supply a DVD player do not expect guests to bring their own DVDs. You should provide a reasonable range of DVDs that will appeal to your target market of guests. About 50 DVDs of various genres will provide a good degree of choice.

Wi-Fi

Wi-Fi is essential and is expected by guests. You will lose bookings if you do not have it. Our experience is that Wi-Fi pays for itself when considering the amount of bookings that would be lost without it.

Coffee/Side Tables

One of the ways you can reduce spillages on couches and chairs (as well as to make your guests' lives easier) is to provide side tables near couches or armchairs. If you have wood floors make sure that they have surface protectors on the feet to prevent scratches.

Bookcase/Shelving/Storage

A storage area for books, magazines, CDs, DVDs and board games is recommended. Books and magazines not only create a homely feel but guests who have a bit more time than they normally would will enjoy leafing through them. To prevent your house from looking like a doctor's surgery, be sure to refresh magazines quarterly (or buy lifestyle magazines which aren't dated on the front).

Music

Portable Bluetooth speakers are the ideal choice for holiday rentals as they are easy to operate. This way guests can enjoy music from their mobile devices, even outside.

Pictures/Photos/Artwork

There is a balance to be had when decorating your walls. Not enough and your property will look stark and unfinished, and too many it will look cluttered and unkempt. Find a balance of art or pictures – a rough guide is one to two good-sized pictures per room. Try to have art or pictures that reflect the area around you. Local photographers are often keen to showcase their works for free in return for a little advertising at the property.

You should remove any personal/family photos and valuable items from your property.

Ornaments

Avoid the temptation to fill your holiday rental full of knick-knacks. A few small ornaments that reflect the local area are fine, but any more than a few makes your property look untidy. Keep any ornaments out of the reach of small children and the wagging tails of passing dogs.

Lamps

Provide a range of lighting options for your guests to create different areas to relax in. That snugly armchair will need a reading light and ceiling lights can be brash whilst watching TV. Dimmer switches can also be a good way to create ambiance.

Fireplace

If you have a fireplace at your property don't skimp by not providing wood, firelighters, kindling, newspapers and matches.

You should obtain a full load of firewood each year and keep this in a shed in the garden so that guests don't run out of wood. Be sure to have your cleaners check regularly so you can have another load delivered before the logs run out.

You will also need to supply equipment to tend the fire (brush, poker and basket or bucket for supplies). A fire guard is also recommended.

An owner says ...

If guests haven't had much experience with lighting fires they will use too much kindling and you will run out quickly, leading to complaints. If you can, have your cleaner set up the fire so that the guest simply has to light it with a match. This also helps the guest to understand how to set up the fire without using too much kindling.

Dining Room

Dining Table and Chairs

Carefully select a table that fits with the theme of your property – whether it be a rustic country cottage or a whitewashed beach theme. If you are short on space consider an expanding table that can fold away when not in use.

Your property should have enough seats for everyone to sit down and eat dinner at the same time. A couple of different areas to sit down and eat at is acceptable.

High Chair

To be family friendly, this is a must have. A folding high chair that can be stored when not in use is a good option.

Bedrooms

Single Beds

Where you only have room for a single bed, consider bunk beds to provide room for an extra person. Trundle beds can also be good for kids rooms.

Queen Beds

Never buy a double bed unless you do not have the space required for a queen bed. Queen beds provide an acceptable level of comfort for both sleepers. Avoid cheap metal-framed beds or budget furniture. Invest in quality such as timber beds.

If you do have to buy a double bed make sure it does not have a bed end at the foot of the bed. This will allow taller guests to hang their feet off the end of the bed rather than being crushed up.

Bunk Beds

Bunk beds can be a great way to increase the capacity of your holiday rental property particularly if you have children staying. Kids love bunk beds – adults will tolerate sleeping in bunk beds as long as they are full-sized, king singles or doubles (tri-bunk). Again, avoid cheap metal bunk beds that create a budget look.

Make sure that bunk beds have secure ladders (and check these periodically). You may also find that bunk beds require tightening of bolts at least once a year due to the movement of guests in the upper bunk.

Mattresses

One of the most important factors to get right is the mattress. Given that guests preferences will vary, seek to buy mattresses that are of reasonable quality and medium softness.

Pillows

Two pillows should be provided for each single bed and four for queen beds. Avoid very cheap pillows and select medium height. Have extra pillows available. If you have your own pillows that you don't want guests to use you should lock them away with your personal items because guests will find them and use them.

Bedside Tables

Where you have a bed, have two bedside tables. Guests need the convenience of having somewhere to lay a book or a pair of glasses at night. Closed bedside tables with drawers are preferable as this prevents dusty shelves and reduces cleaning required. For guest comfort always make sure bedside tables are higher than the top of the mattress.

An owner says ...

We kept finding alarm clock radios unplugged and hidden in drawers. It was obvious that they were unpopular with guests. We decided to swap them for universal chargers for smartphones which proved infinitely more popular.

Bedside Lamps

Bedside lamps should always be supplied if space is available. Guests have more time on their hands on holiday and may choose to read in bed or relax in the bedroom.

Bedrooms can act as an escape from other friends or family if required. Lamps provide a convenient alternative to ceiling lights that can be glaring. Bedside lamps also give a bedroom a balanced, finished look.

Wardrobes

Always have a place for guests to hang their clothes and drawers to store other clothes in. If you have guests staying for a week or longer, try to ensure that the wardrobe has sufficient capacity to store a week's worth of clothes for each person in the room. If you do not have sufficient space a small rack may be acceptable. All hanging space should have at least twelve coat hangers.

You should also remove your personal belongings from wardrobes.

Chair

Where possible provide a chair for guests in the bedroom to make it easier for them to put shoes on or simply to have another seat to relax in. Many beds are too high to put shoes on easily.

TV

A TV in the bedroom (with Netflix) may be useful for larger properties where guests may wish to have some separation from other guests in order to have privacy.

Powerboards

If you don't have power points next to each bedside cabinet (i.e. two) be sure to supply power boards so that guests can charge their phones and other gadgets. Installing a few extra power points can make things more convenient for guests and reduce the amount of unattractive power cables on display.

Blankets/Throws

If you are in an area that gets cold, extra blankets/throws are recommended for the winter months.

Fans

If you are in an area that gets hot, and particularly if there is no air conditioning in the bedrooms, a fan in each bedroom (either ceiling or pedestal) can help keep guests comfortable. Ceiling fans or wall mounted fans are ideal if you are short of floor space. Pedestal fans are easily broken, so if your budget permits go for a ceiling fan with a remote control (for extra guest convenience). Be sure to have spare batteries for the remote control easily accessible.

Fans also get dusty very quickly so be sure to have your cleaners check these at least once a month.

Heaters

If there is no heating in bedrooms and it's likely to get cold, a small heater in each bedroom (such as a fin oil column heater) is a good idea. If short of space a combined heater/fan is a good choice (e.g. Dyson). If you choose to install gas heaters make sure you also install a carbon monoxide detector.

Portacot

To be family friendly you must have a portacot (also known as a travel crib). Portacots can fold up to fit in a wardrobe or slide under most beds so they don't take up much room.

Kitchen

The secret to a great kitchen in a holiday rental is to provide everything a guest would need at home to create basic dishes. A common mistake amongst holiday rental owners is to only provide limited facilities. This can be very frustrating for guests who want to eat in – particularly those that have pets that they cannot take to a restaurant. Remember that your guests may also be choosing to stay at your holiday rental to save money by not having to eat out.

A guest says ...

We once stayed at a 3-bedroom apartment. It was lovely but the kitchen had no pots and pans and there were only four sets of plates, glasses, cups, bowls and cutlery. With there being six of us we had to eat in two sittings, washing up in between! It was a terrible experience that could have been so easily avoided. We left a very grumpy review on Tripadvisor.

Appliances

Essential appliances include:

- fridge/freezer
- oven/stove
- dishwasher
- 4-slice toaster (please do your guests a favour and don't buy a 2-slice toaster!)
- kettle
- microwave
- espresso machine (pod machines are simple to use but cost more in the long run).

Where possible, download a copy of the appliance manual from the web, save it to an online cloud drive (Google Drive is ideal) and include a link to it from the online Guest Guidebook. Paper manuals should be stored on the premises in case of emergency.

A guest says ...

We couldn't get the dishwasher to work. We suddenly imagined our holiday spent washing dishes – disaster! On consulting the online Guest Guidebook we saw that there were instructions on how to reset the machine. It took us 30 seconds to get it working again. Phew!

When buying appliances check that there are service technicians available in the area. More obscure brands may only have technicians in city areas – you could be left waiting for weeks for a costly repair.

An owner says ...

Guests broke the air glider on our air conditioning unit. It took weeks for us to find a technician and then the repair cost us $380 because it was an obscure brand with no service agents for 50km.

Crockery

With crockery aim to have twice as many as your maximum capacity. That is, a house which sleeps eight guests should have sixteen of everything.

For plates and bowls, white crockery is recommended.

Buy both cereal bowls and larger salad bowls.

Don't forget dishwasher safe plastic plates, bowls and cutlery if your guests commonly include kids.

Glasses

Large glasses for soft drinks or beer.

Wine Glasses

Have plenty of these as they will get broken. Avoid delicate glasses.

Pans

Pots and pans (with lids), frying pans.

Cutlery

Forks, knives, dessert spoons, teaspoons, steak knives, a good set of kitchen knives and a sharpener to keep them in good order.

Others

Colander, sieve, whisk, spatulas, BBQ tools, sharp knives, peeler, chopping boards, oven trays/dishes, Tupperware tubs, bottle opener, can opener, containers (for tea, coffee, sugar), dish rack, place mats, tea towels (ten) and soap dispenser are essentials.

Bathrooms

Shower Caddy

If there isn't inbuilt storage in the shower ensure your guests have somewhere to put their soap, shampoo, etc.

Soap Dispenser

Have a pump soap dispenser for hand washing at the sink/hand basin.

Toilet Brush

Always have a toilet brush.

Toilet Roll Holder

Have this in an obvious place so guests don't have to play 'hunt the toilet paper'.

Storage

Make sure you have enough space for guests to put out their toiletries. If not, invest in additional storage or shelving.

Air Freshener

Provide an air freshener block as well as a spray can.

Toilet Blu

A supply of Toilet Blu is essential to keep toilets fresh.

Hair Dryer

One per bathroom.

Laundry

Whilst a separate room for a laundry may be necessary at home you can conserve space by having a European-style laundry with only a washing machine and tumble dryer. Sinks and wash tubs aren't necessary.

Iron and Ironing Board

A basic iron and ironing board are sufficient.

Washing Machine and Dryer

A washing machine and dryer are no longer optional – they are essentials for any holiday rental. You don't need to buy expensive ones. Basic models are satisfactory as long as they are in good working condition.

If you are really short of space, consider a combined washer/dryer. Be aware that these machines can take a long time to dry clothes – often several hours – which can be very inconvenient for your guests.

Other Cleaning Items

Have a vacuum cleaner (bagless recommended), bucket, mop, broom and clothes drying rack (even if you have a washing line).

Tool Kit

When you visit your property you will often find items that need maintenance or repairs so it's a good idea to have a small, well-equipped tool kit handy in the event that you need to tighten screws, glue things or tighten up that furniture with an allen key. You may even find that some guests will fix things themselves.

Labeller

Also useful if you have to add the odd label to lights or appliances to prevent guest confusion. Over time these fade or peel and need regular replacement, so have an electronic labeller (always with waterproof print tape) so that you can keep things up to date. Just don't go crazy and label everything as too many signs create a poor guest experience.

A guest says ...

We turned up at a house that had signs and labels everywhere. We felt like we were being nagged by them wherever we looked. There was even one asking us to close the fridge door. It created a very inhospitable welcome.

Decks/Patios/Verandas

Dining Setting

As per your internal dining, make sure you have adequate seating for your maximum guest capacity.

Remember that you may not be able to visit the property as frequently as you'd like so avoid settings made of materials that require regular maintenance. For example, if the setting is in an area exposed to a lot of sunlight, avoid wood furniture that requires regular oiling and in beachside areas avoid metals that will corrode due to the sea air. Do not use cheap, plastic furniture.

Outdoor Lounge

If space and climate permits, an outdoor area for relaxing can be a great feature to attract guests. Outdoor lounges, daybeds, hammocks, sun lounges or just comfortable chairs provide ideal spots for guests to relax.

In some areas it may be necessary to cover your furniture to ensure that it is not damaged by the elements or to prevent it from becoming dusty. Vinyl covers can be a good way of protecting your furniture, but they should be tied down to prevent them blowing away in strong winds. As properties become more popular and are therefore being cleaned more regularly it may not be necessary to cover furniture (and covering/uncovering furniture will be one less thing for guests to worry about).

BBQ

A BBQ is essential for properties in warm climates where alfresco dining is the norm. If you are located at a coastal area, be mindful that cheaper steel BBQs will rust rapidly in the sea air. Be sure to buy a BBQ that can cater adequately for the maximum capacity of the holiday rental.

To keep your BBQ in good shape, supply your guests with BBQ cleaning products, a robust BBQ brush and drip trays (if required).

Always have two gas cylinders to prevent guests running out of gas (if you are using bottled gas).

Hose

A small hose on a reel is sufficient for guests to hose down dogs, cars or boats without taking up too much space.

Lighting

Be sure to install adequate lighting in outdoor areas. If the weather permits, guests love spending time in outdoor areas, especially at night.

Consider installing an LED sensor light for your front door so that guests can get in easily if they arrive at night. A small torch on a hook next to your lock box is also an option but this will require regular replacement of batteries and the torches often mysteriously disappear!

Also ensure that any areas that represent a trip hazard are well lit, such as exterior stairs or pathways. Solar powered lights can also be a useful option.

Bug Protection

If your property is in an area that has lots of bugs (e.g. mosquitoes) consider installing a bug zapper. Avoid cheap battery powered ones or ones that plug in and purchase a good quality one that can be hard-wired and placed out of guests' reach (to avoid kids fingers).

Keys/Keyless Entry

Keyless entry systems replace the door lock and mean that the guest simply has to enter a code to open the door.

These systems are definitely worth the extra cost due to their convenience for guests and the fact that you'll never have to worry about keys again!

Keyless entry systems range from basic manual systems to electronic locks that you can program remotely.

Lock Box

A lock box with a combination is a low cost, easy-to-use option, but is not as convenient as a keyless entry system.

If you do go for a lock box, ensure that you have a minimum of four sets of keys:

1. One to keep in your lock box
2. One hidden at the property for when your guests lock the keys inside (it will happen)

3. One for the cleaners (or an additional cleaner lock box which some cleaners prefer – this also means you don't have to hide a key at the property)

4. One to keep at home.

An owner says ...

Do your guests a favour and put your lock box next to the front door for convenience. Yes, someone could smash it and take the key but this would probably be more difficult than breaking down the door!

CCTV Cameras

Whilst under no circumstances should you install a CCTV camera inside your property, there may be some situations where cameras are warranted in exterior areas. Examples could include external areas where noise needs to be kept to a minimum (where you may need evidence of guests breaking rules) or for properties that have had incidences of theft in the past. Cameras should only be installed as a last resort as they could put guests off booking.

It's advisable to have any cameras hard wired as well as connected to your Wi-Fi so that you can view footage remotely.

If you do decide to install a CCTV camera on the exterior of your property you should follow some simple rules:

1. You must inform guests on the booking websites that there are security cameras at the property. State clearly why they are present.

2. You must provide signage at the property informing guests that they may be recorded on CCTV

3. Do not install cameras in areas such as decks or patios where guests spend a great deal of time and where the cameras will be

construed as an invasion of privacy. Ideally install the cameras at the front of the property at access points.

If you are in any doubt, it is best not to install a CCTV system.

An owner says ...

We suspected that neighbours were stealing wood from our shed during the quiet winter months. We installed a CCTV camera at the front of our property and the theft stopped almost immediately.

Alarm Systems

You should never ask guests to switch alarm systems on and off as it is simply too much of an inconvenience for them. As a result an alarm system should only be installed if you are planning on using the property yourself for an extended period of time or are closing up the property for months at a time during low season.

Other Recommended Facilities

Games Console

For family-friendly holidays a games console can keep little kids (and big kids) amused. Be sure to supply a good range of games. To prevent guests from churning through batteries it is better to supply wired controllers.

Toys

If you are aiming to be family friendly, have a couple of tubs full of toys that cater for both girls and boys. If you have large outdoor areas (such as a carport), ride-on kids toys can also provide hours of amusement.

Think about toys that will enhance the guest experience. For example, boogie boards and buckets and spades for the beach or even a set of family bicycles (with helmets).

If supplying ride-on toys or equipment, make sure that your insurance policy covers any loss or accidents.

Pool/Table Tennis Tables

Pool tables or table tennis are great if you have adequate space. Be sure to have an adequate supply of bats, balls, pool cues and chalk. Check these regularly as they do deteriorate with use.

Board Games

Board games are great for holidays when guests have a little more time than normal. Jigsaws can be fun for kids and adults alike.

Binoculars/Telescope

If your property has good views or if there is interesting wildlife in the area guests will appreciate having these. Be sure to label the binoculars with your property name to prevent them from being taken home by accident.

Pets

30% of travellers* are looking for holiday rentals that accept pets, therefore it's strongly recommended that your property is pet friendly. To be a pet-friendly property you should meet a few simple requirements:

- Allow pets inside
- Have a fully enclosed garden
- Supply water bowls and dog toys (replace toys regularly).

If you don't have a fully enclosed garden this doesn't exclude you from accepting pets so long as you clearly communicate the limitations to guests prior to booking.

It's recommended that you supply guests with pets a list of pet-friendly rules that they must adhere to so that the property is left in perfect condition.

For example:
- Please do not let dogs on couches or beds
- Please clean up excessive amounts of dog hair
- We are a child-friendly property so please pick up all doggy doos
- Please put dog toys back in the box and don't mix them up with the kids toys
- Please don't take the dog toys home with you
- Please put dog bowls back where you found them
- If your dog chews anything to death please put it in the bin!

Source: HomeAway

Linen

Supplying linen at your property is absolutely essential, particularly if you regularly have overseas guests. Linen is now mandatory on Airbnb and it's likely that the other booking websites will follow suit.

Have three sets of *white* linen. This will prevent your cleaners having to wash linen on busy changeover days. White is a good option as it can be washed at high temperatures and bleached to remove tough stains (aside from the fact that it looks clean and inviting).

Linen should be stored in a locked cupboard that the cleaners can easily access to prevent guests helping themselves and pushing up your cleaning costs!

To stop cleaners from losing your linen by mixing it up with other properties, you can mark it with the property name and size of linen (e.g. Single, Queen, King, etc.) Make sure you use a proper linen marker pen.

For an efficient process, have the cleaners make up all of the beds and set out towels for each stay at every clean. This means that the property will always be ready for guests (and will prevent those last minute booking panics). Make sure that your communications with guests specify that guests may use a number of beds equal to the number of guests on the booking and that extra fees will apply if the number of beds used exceeds the number of guests.

For example, if four adults book the property and six beds are used you will be entitled to charge an extra fee for the additional two beds used. This will prevent guests trying to pull the wool over your eyes by bringing more guests than is stated on the reservation.

If extra beds are used you should ask your cleaners to provide photographic evidence (on the day of check-out).

Sheets

Provide both a fitted sheet and a top sheet for each bed. Ensure sheets are of reasonable quality (check the thread count). 250 thread count is acceptable for budget properties, but at least 500 thread count is recommended for all others.

Pillowcases

You will need one pillowcase per single bed and two per double/queen bed. The remaining pillowcases can be supplied as part of the doona sets. You should ask guests not to use the pillows supplied with the doona set in order to keep them fresh.

Protectors

Ensure you buy mattress and pillow protectors, as they will help keep your mattresses and pillows stain and odour free. Make sure your cleaners wash these regularly.

You will need two sets of protectors per bed.

Towels

You will need three sets of towels x your maximum guest numbers. Also three bathmats and two hand towels per bathroom.

Darker colours are recommended for towels as stains do not display as easily.

Doona Sets

Each bed will need two doona sets and one doona. A doona set comprises doona cover and two pillowcases. A spare doona of each size is recommended per property in case one needs to be washed.

Choose doona sets that match if multiple beds are in the same room as this creates a nice effect, particularly in your photos. It is also a good idea to buy two identical doona covers per bed. This way if one doona cover is dirty then the cleaners can swap over one cover rather than having to swap over all four to keep the room looking uniform.

Garish colours or designs should be avoided. Throw pillows can also add a nice touch.

Fire Safety

Check your local regulations to ensure that you are meeting all the requirements for fire safety. Regulations aside you should have a working smoke alarm on each level of the property (and spare batteries available) as well as a small fire extinguisher and fire blanket located in the kitchen near the stove. If you have gas fires a carbon monoxide detector should also be installed.

Consumables/Pantry Items

Consumables are the items in your property which guests actually use, or consume.

Many holiday rentals skimp on consumable items. This is a mistake as they do not cost a lot of money to supply and can make a big difference to the guest experience.

Ideally, buy in bulk and re-stock your property every three to six months. Here's a list of the essential items to supply:

Kitchen:

Item	Bought?
Scourers (yellow sponge with green scourer)	
Hand soap (liquid)	
Dishwasher powder and rinse aid	
Dishwashing liquid	
Coffee: instant	
Coffee: ground (or pods for pod espresso machine: 20 per booking)	
Tea bags	
Sugar	
Olive oil	
Balsamic vinegar	
Tomato sauce	
Item	**Bought?**
BBQ sauce	
Salt	
Pepper	
Aluminium foil	
Gladwrap	
Baking paper	
Wipes (for wiping down kitchen benches and spills)	
Bin bags	
Carpet stain remover	
Insect repellant (if required)	
Bug spray	
First aid kit	
Batteries (AAA for remote controls/9V for smoke alarms)	
Spare light globes (not required if using LED's)	

Living Area/Bedrooms:

Item	Bought
Tissues (one in living area, one in each bedroom)	

Bathroom:

Item	Bought
Shampoo	
Hair conditioner	
Shower gel	
Toilet Blu	
Toilet paper (three rolls per toilet)	
Air fresheners/sprays	

Laundry:

Item	Bought
Laundry powder	
Laundry liquid	

It is a good idea to tell your cleaners to stock up on any items that are running low (and to understand what they will charge you to do this). Whilst many properties put consumable items under lock and key for fear of theft, this is unnecessary. Guests are, on the whole, honest and respectful and will not pillage your home!

An owner says ...

Even though our area was not affected a large fire caused the government to shut our local area as a precaution. This meant that we had to cancel two of our bookings. We were able to claim on our insurance policy for loss of rent which saved us five thousand dollars.

Garbage Bins

You'd be surprised at how much garbage guests can generate whilst on holiday (particularly the amount of bottles of booze they drink).

To ensure your bins don't overflow and become stinky, as a rough guide the following will provide enough capacity:

- 1 x 240L General Waste Bin
- 2 x 240L Recycling Bins

Depending on your local council, extra bins may incur a fee – it is certainly worth paying a little extra to avoid guests turning up to find overflowing bins and the stench of rotting garbage.

In the event that you do have a situation with overflowing bins, have a process in place for your cleaners to dispose of excess garbage before the next guests arrive.

It is a good idea to add signage near both your main interior bin and your exterior bins to advise guests of bin collection days. It's also a good idea to add this to your Guest Guidebook.

Occasionally you'll find that guests simply create an unreasonable level of garbage. In these events it's important that your rental agreement or rules state that there will be charges for excess garbage.

An owner says ...

Our rules state that if the guests use more than a full bin then they will be charged for excess garbage removal. We also ask guests to inform us if the bin is more than two thirds full on arrival so that we can arrange to take garbage away.

Damage and Extra Fees

If guests cause damage to the property or if extra cleaning tasks are required your cleaners should provide photographic evidence on the day of the clean. Most of the booking websites give you 48 hours to claim extra fees from the guest. This isn't always a straightforward process so be prepared to produce photographic evidence of damage or items that will incur extra fees (e.g. extra cleaning tasks) as well as receipts in the event of items damaged.

It really isn't worth the effort to claim for small amounts of damage such as broken glasses, and of course you cannot claim for general wear and tear.

An owner says ...

Keep every receipt of anything you've ever bought for your property. A guest had a nosebleed on one of our beds destroying a doona cover. The booking website asked us to provide proof of the value of the item. Luckily we had kept the receipt and were able to receive compensation.

Staff

Unless you live close to your property, you'll require some staff to maintain and clean the property for you. If you do live close to the property and are planning on doing this yourself, be mindful of the amount of work required to both clean and maintain a property and whether it is worth your time to do so. Cleaners remain one of the lowest paid occupations.

Whatever staff you choose to work with always, always have at least two of each type on your list of contacts. People may go on holiday, move areas or get sick, so you need to have multiple options for when an emergency strikes.

An owner says ...

We hadn't had a bill from our lawn mowing guy for a while. Turns out he had a heart attack and was in hospital! Luckily our cleaners helped out by mowing lawns until he got better. Since then we've always made sure we have a backup.

Agreements and Contracts

Whatever staff you engage it's always best to have a professionally written contract or agreement specifying the terms of the engagement. This doesn't have to be a legal contract drawn up in triplicate – it just needs to set out expectations and fees clearly.

Here are some of the jobs that you may need to employ staff to do at your property:

- Cleaning
- Lawns and garden care
- Repairs and maintenance
- Plumbing
- Electrical installation/repairs.

Let's look at each of those in order.

Cleaning

Guests these days expect the highest standards of cleanliness to be demonstrated at holiday rentals irrespective of the quality of the property. Therefore it is vitally important that you select the right cleaner (or cleaning company). So how do you go about hiring the right one?

1. Ask the cleaner what experience they have and ask them to supply references. Anyone can become a cleaner but not everyone does a good job at it!

2. Ask them how many holiday rentals they clean in the area. As a rough guide an average holiday rental (three bedrooms) will take 3–4 hours to clean.

Bear in mind that if you hire a cleaner that works on their own they will only be able to clean up to a small 3-bedroom home on their own during a 4-hour booking window (assuming they are also changing linen). If they are cleaning multiple properties ask them if they have assistance to complete two cleans at the same time if there is a check-out on the same day. This often catches out solo cleaners. Do not, under any circumstances agree to block calendars so that cleaners have extra time to clean – this will cost you thousands in lost bookings. Always be clear with cleaners that the clean must be completed in the 4-hour cleaning window on the day of check-out. 11am to 3pm is ideal.

3. Ask them where they live. The closer they are to your holiday rental the better. That way they can assist with any last minute issues that guests may have (and make sure bins are put out when required).

4. If you are supplying linen and towels be sure to ask how much they charge per bed or per bundle of towels (or even a fixed price to do everything).

5. Walk them through the property showing them where you keep supplies and linen. If you can't be there in person provide them with access via your lock box and ask them to call or Skype/FaceTime you so you can walk them through it (you can always change your lock box code afterwards).

6. Many cleaners will also mow lawns, keep gardens tidy and perform maintenance – ask them what other tasks they can perform. It can be more convenient to have them do all of the jobs and it means less invoices to pay.

7. Ensure that they have an email address that they check daily. With online property bookings being the norm, you should not have to text or call them. Also ensure that they provide their mobile num-

ber(s) in case of emergency.

8. Ask them if they have a checklist that they follow – many may not have this but if you find a cleaner that employs a checklist it is a good sign that they are focused on quality.

9. Ask them if they have a back-up for when they go on holiday or if they are sick.

10. Ask them if they are happy to be your 'emergency contact' in the event that something goes wrong. This is particularly important if you do not live near the property (and even if you do live nearby wouldn't you rather they did it?) Whilst issues are rare you always need a person available to attend in person (quickly) if a situation arises.

Whether they have a checklist or not you should always document what your expectations are with regard to cleaning tasks. Make clear what you require done at each clean as well as cleaning tasks performed weekly, monthly, quarterly or annually.

Try to avoid the complication of hourly rates and different prices per clean by agreeing either:

Set fee per clean including linen or

Set fee per clean plus an additional fee per bed (this may vary depending on the size of bed).

An owner says ...

We got into a difficult situation with a cleaner who was on an hourly rate. She was spending so much time at the property that our cleaning costs started to skyrocket. Upon further investigation we found out that she was performing excessive and unnecessarily cleaning tasks to try to improve her income. We created a checklist clarifying exactly what was required per clean and switched her onto a fixed fee per clean which resolved the problem.

When taking on a new cleaner it's a good idea to do a test run. If possible, create a booking under a fake name but stay at the property yourself. Add a couple of tests such as crumbs spilled on the couch, a stain on the benchtop or a smear of sauce on the wall to check attention to detail. If the cleaner passes the test then check in with the next guests to see if the standards are being maintained. Some cleaners have a habit of starting off well and relaxing their standards as they become more comfortable with the property. Keep a close eye on reviews and check the property carefully each time you visit to ensure that nothing is being missed. Invest in quarterly spring cleans to keep the property in top condition.

It's important to document what your cleaning standards are explicitly. What is clean to one person may not be clean to another.

It's also important that both you and you cleaning staff monitor your stocks of consumable items.

An owner says ...

We hired a new cleaner and after a month noticed that our stock of items was depleting rapidly! It was clear to us that the cleaner was helping herself to items intended for the guests. We very quickly replaced her and there were no further issues. It's important to vet cleaners carefully and always ask for references.

Lawns and Garden Care

If your cleaners don't look after lawns and gardens then be sure to find someone who does. Make sure that their brief includes mowing lawns and edges as well as trimming bushes and taking care of weeds.

Make sure that any gardeners you use are aware that their brief includes mowing lawns and edges, blowing leaves away as well as trimming bushes and taking care of weeds.

Be sure to set up a regular schedule for mowing. Guests turning up to an unkempt garden is not a good first impression. Ensure that your lawn mowing staff are booked into regular schedules for mowing rather than asking for your go-ahead each time. This way your lawns and garden will always look their best for guests arriving.

If you want to keep costs down, you could ask your staff to send you a photo prior to mowing so that you can give the OK as to whether the mow is required but over time you will get a feel as to what mowing or maintenance frequency is required.

There's nothing worse than guests being woken up by a lawn mower at 7am on a Sunday morning after a big night, so ensure that your gardening staff have view-only access to your booking calendar. If your booking systems don't provide this option then you may have to ask your staff to check with you before each mow, or at least to check if there are obvious signs that guests are there (e.g. cars parked in the driveway).

An owner says ...

We hired a gardener to do our lawns and edges and whilst they did a great job they didn't consider weeding as part of their job! After finding our garden beds and paths covered in weeds we decided to find someone else who would do everything for us.

Repairs and Maintenance

When that curtain rod falls down or a door handle falls off you'll be needing someone to fix it quickly so that you can minimise the impact to guests. When selecting someone to do this, get them to provide a list of things that they can assist with. Whilst maintenance is not generally a large ongoing expense you will have small repair jobs that will need to be done over the years.

An owner says ...

Some of the repairs that we have had to do include replacing fly screens, fixing door handles, repairing sticking windows, fixing loose screws on chairs and roller blinds that no longer roll. Maintenance isn't a large expense at our property but it is important to fix things as soon as there is an issue with them. Over time, small niggles that remain unfixed multiply to create a poor impression on guests which then leads to negative reviews.

Plumbing

Plumbing problems are likely to be infrequent, but blocked drains, dripping taps, faulty toilets or a failed hot water system can ruin a guest's stay. Again look for a plumber that is close at hand and who is readily contactable 24/7.

An owner says ...

We got a call at 10pm at night, when a pipe had burst under the house. Luckily our plumber was out there in 15 minutes to fix the problem. We had selected him as he was close by and was happy to come out at any hour.

Electrical Installations/Repairs

Electrical repairs are uncommon but they do happen. Guests sitting in the dark is not something that you even want to think about! As per plumbers, look for an electrician that is close at hand and who is readily contactable 24/7.

When first setting up the property you may find that you need extra sockets behind beds for lamps. You should also look to install a circuit breaker, particularly if you have young children staying at the property.

Insurance

It is a common misconception that general insurers adequately cover short-term holiday rental properties. Be very careful to ensure that your insurance gives you complete coverage and specifies 'short-term rentals'.

Having tailored holiday rental insurance is essential in order to protect both you and your guests. If you fail to have adequate cover you are exposing yourself and your guests to unnecessary risk. Here's what a good holiday rental insurance policy should include:

Building and Contents

As per your usual home insurance you should make sure that you have both building and contents insurance. You should also check that your contents insurance covers malicious damage in the unlikely event that someone wilfully causes damage to your property. Don't worry – this is very unlikely!

Accidental/Malicious Damage

Malicious damage refers to a guest willfully damaging a property such as the old rock star cliche of throwing a TV out of a window!

Accidental damage refers to damage done that is not wilful. It is very important to have accidental damage cover as this is more likely to be the cause of damage at a holiday rental than malicious damage.

An owner says…

We had guests that were attending a wedding and had bought some confetti. It was a wet day and their kids were playing with the confetti inside. The coloured confetti fell on our wood floor and due to the wet conditions stained the floors causing ten thousand dollars worth of damage. We were lucky that we had accidental damage insurance as the damage was not caused maliciously.

Public Liability

Public liability insurance provides protection for you in the event that a guest is injured on your property. It is your legal protection if you are found to be responsible for personal injury to a visitor at your property (including both guests and others).

Loss of Rent

In the event that your holiday rental property is unavailable for rent due to an insured event (e.g. flood, fire, etc.) loss of rent cover will pay for the loss of rent that you incur up to a specified amount.

An owner says ...

Even though our area was not affected, a large fire caused the government to shut our local area as a precaution. This meant that we had to cancel two of our bookings. We were able to claim on our insurance policy for loss of rent which saved us five thousand dollars.

Prior to moving on to set up your online listings, use the following checklist to ensure that you have your property fully set up:

Set-up Checklist

Staff	Hired?
Cleaners	
Lawns and Garden Care	
Maintenance	
Plumber	
Electrician	

Insurance

Staff	Hired?
Building and Contents	
Accidental/Malicious Damage	
Public Liability	
Loss of Rent	

Furniture and Appliances

Room	Item	Purchased?
Single Bedroom #1	Bunk beds	
	Single mattress	
	Foam trundle mattress	
	Storage drawers/wardrobe	
	Heater	
	Fan	
	Kids toys/books	
Single Bedroom #2	Bunk beds	
	Single mattress	
	Foam trundle mattress	
	Storage drawers/wardrobe	
	Heater	
	Fan	
	Kids toys/books	
Queen Bedroom #1	Queen bed	
	Storage drawers/wardrobe	
	Queen mattress	
	Bedside tables	
	Bedside lamps	
	Wardrobe	
	Heater	
	Fan	
Queen Bedroom #2	Queen bed	
	Storage drawers/wardrobe	
	Queen mattress	
	Bedside tables	
	Bedside lamps	
	Wardrobe	
	Heater	
	Fan	

Room	Item	Purchased?
Queen Bedroom #3	Queen bed	
	Storage drawers/wardrobe	
	Queen mattress	
	Bedside tables	
	Bedside lamps	
	Wardrobe	
	Heater	
	Fan	
Living Room	Couch(es)	
	TV	
	DVD	
	Games console	
	Wi-Fi router	
	Coffee/side tables	
	Rug	
	Bar stools	
	TV unit	
	Stereo system	
	Pictures/photos/artwork	
	Ornaments	
	Floor lamp/table lamp	
	Guest book	

Room	Item	Purchased?
Kitchen	Plates (large/small)	
	Kids plates/bowls	
	Bowls	
	Glasses	
	Wine glasses	
	Pans	
	Utensils	
	Knives	
	Tea, coffee, sugar holders	
	Cutlery	
	Toaster	
	Bin	
	Kettle	
	Mugs	
	Chopping boards	
	Fridge/freezer	
	Soap dispenser	
	Dish rack	
	Plastic storage tubs	
	Dishwasher	
	Stove and oven	
	Coffee machine	
	Microwave	
Bathroom	Toilet brush	
	Soap dispenser	
	Shower caddy	

Room	Item	Purchased?
Laundry	Washing machine	
	Tumble dryer	
	Laundry basket	
	Clothes pegs	
	Vacuum cleaner	
	Portacot	
	Ironing board	
	High chair	
	Iron	
	Brush and pan	
	Mop and bucket	
Patio	Table setting	
	Outdoor lounge	
	BBQ	
	Hot plate, brush and cover	
	BBQ gas	
	Dog toys and bowls (for pet-friendly properties)	
	Key safe/keys	
Linen	Doona sets	
	Doonas	
	Single sets	
	Pillows	
	Pillowcases	
	Queen sets	
	Mattress protectors	
	Pillow protectors	
	Blankets	

Room	Item	Purchased?
Consumables / Pantry Items	Toilet paper	
	Hand soap	
	Dishwasher powder	
	Rinse aid	
	Dishwashing Liquid	
	Coffee – instant	
	Coffee – ground	
	Tea bags	
	Sugar	
	Olive oil	
	Balsamic vinegar	
	Tomato sauce	
	BBQ sauce	
	Salt	
	Pepper	
	Cloths	
	Scrubbers	
	Tissues	
	Air fresheners (both toilets)	
	Toilet Blu	
	Insect spray	
	Insect repellent	
	Laundry powder	
	Stain remover	
	Bin bags	

PART 3:

Listing Your Property for Rental

So you've finished setting up your property. Now for the exciting part – letting the world in ... and making money!

Naming Your Property

One of your first decisions will be to think up a name for your holiday rental. This isn't as simple as it may sound. Remember that something too difficult to spell may be hard for people to locate online and something too generic may get lost in the sea of other properties. Try a search for properties called 'Mountain View' or 'The Beach Shack' and you'll find an overwhelming amount of similarly named properties. You may also wish to check if the web address for your chosen name is available prior to settling on a name (you can do this by searching for 'domain name providers' on Google and plugging in your chosen name ideas on their website). It's good to keep your property name short as it will allow you more space to add key features of your property to the title in the booking websites (more about that later).

Telling Your Story

It can be nice to weave in local or family history into the name of your property. It creates something memorable. When we bought our first holiday rental, Hayes Beach House, we included the story of how we found our property in our guide book. Stories capture the imagination of guests. When we were featured on a national Australian radio station they told the story about how the house was named after our family home in the Shetland Islands of Scotland.

It's Your Home Too!

It's sometimes easy to focus on making money and to forget that a holiday rental is about your enjoyment too. As the property gets busier the time you spend at the house may become more difficult to come by. When you get to this stage, sit down and agree with your family as to how much you want to use the property on a monthly or annual basis. Plan ahead and book time in your calendar as you would for a guest.

An owner says ...

It became an emotional dilemma for us to stay at our house during summer as we knew that we were losing money when we decided to stay. After a while we found that we were missing the place terribly and decided to bite the bullet and go down once a month regularly. Despite the bonus of the extra income it was very important to enjoy it ourselves too. We didn't buy it just for the money.

Avoiding Common Mistakes

Before talking about all the things you need to do to get the property listed online, let's tackle some of the key mistakes that holiday rental owners make. Once you recognise these you can prevent yourself from making serious errors when you do list your property.

Responding Too Slowly or Not At All

When guests look for a holiday rental if they do not wish to book instantly they may submit several enquiries within a short timeframe so they can compare responses from the different property owners.

The most common problem for holiday rental owners is either responding too slowly (greater than two hours) or not responding at all. Obviously not responding at all is a sure fire way not to get a booking, but the reason for not responding at all is typically that the Owner's Calendar has not been updated when they receive a booking and therefore they see no point in responding to the enquiry. This is a very frustrating experience for the customer who may send several enquiries and receive no response! Speed of response is a competitive differentiator. If you can respond to a customer quicker than anyone else (within 30 minutes using professional templates) your conversion rate will dwarf your competitors. You should also *follow up* with the guest 1–2 days later (something that very few owners do). Owners who do not respond or respond slowly can be penalised by the booking websites – a surefire way for your property to become less visible over time.

Getting Pricing Wrong

There are many factors to pricing but there is nothing more frustrating for a customer than to check a price on the system and then receive a totally different price in the quote from the property. This is typically the result of disorganised owners who struggle to understand how to put pricing into booking systems. This leads to owners having to cancel or decline bookings which has an extremely detrimental effect on the property's rank.

Arguably worse than getting the pricing wrong is when a holiday rental owner prices the property too high or too low. Pricing too high is often an ego-driven response where the owner thinks their property is better than competing properties and leads to extremely low enquiries and conversions. Low-priced properties run the risk of making themselves look like budget properties thereby attracting the wrong standard of clientele. Whilst these properties are likely to book out, they are missing out on tens of thousands of dollars in rental income due to under-pricing.

Poor Photographs

Photographs are the lifeblood of a holiday rental property listing. Whilst guests may choose not to read the property description text, they will *always* look at the photos. Why then, do so many owners post fuzzy, amateurish photos on their listings? The fact of the matter is that they underestimate how impactful professional quality photos are. Whilst taking photos with a smartphone or digital SLR will give you photos that will meet the booking website's standards (typically high resolution), having professional quality photos elevates the property to an entirely new level of appeal. For an incredibly low investment (around $200–300 dollars) professional photos represent the best return on investment you can make. Given that every real estate agent in the world has access to a professional photographer you should have little difficulty finding one!

An owner says ...

We took photos with our digital camera and we sat back, smugly admiring how good we thought they were. When a special offer for professional photography came along we decided to give it a go, more as an experiment than anything else. We were gobsmacked when we saw the quality of the photos compared to ours (which suddenly looked dark and uninviting in comparison).

Poor Descriptions

There is a reason that websites today have tightly written professional text that conveys what they are offering in a few sentences. It's because of the incredibly short attention spans of customers! As a result, descriptions of properties have to convey the best aspects of the property and area to the guest quickly before they lose interest (usually only a few seconds). Typically property owners will write descriptions filled with property facts, rather than conveying the experience that guests are looking for. Property descriptions should evoke emotions rather than only the facts regarding the property. The booking websites all contain detailed property information as standard so adding factual information to the property description fields simply duplicates the information presented.

Avoiding Online Booking Systems

Rather than using online payment systems some owners try to contact guests and ask them to pay direct to bank accounts to avoid booking website fees. Not only does this reduce conversion rate (and consequently the property rank) but this can lead to immediate removal of the property from booking websites.

Not Listing on Effective Websites

The market is dominated by HomeAway, Airbnb and Booking.com and these should be your first port of call when listing your property. These charge a percentage fee of the booking amount.

Avoid website listings with upfront fees unless you have clear evidence from others using the website that you will get a return on your investment.

An owner says ...

In our first couple of years of having our holiday rental property we were somewhat naive and signed up for almost every new holiday rental website that came along – usually for some sort of $99 special upfront payment. After seeing a few of these websites come and go with no return on investment we decided never again to list with a website that charged an upfront fee. We now only list our property with those websites that offer a success based (percentage) fee structure.

Taking the 'Budget Option'

Often you will hear people say, 'Oh it's just a holiday rental, just get some cheap furniture, some lino on the floor and you'll rent it out no problem'. And they are correct ... if you want to receive under $100 a night and to be competing with cheap motels with sticky carpets. Sadly many owners fall into this trap thinking that guests will trash the furniture and not respect the property. From this thinking the owner goes out and picks up second hand furniture and cheap items from discount stores. Taking the budget option leads to a budget price point and attracts the kind of guests who *will* damage your property. By investing in better quality fixtures, fittings and furniture the increased price point that you can charge will pay for the better quality furniture and provide you with increased income. Pitching your property as a budget option is a false economy.

Not Gathering Reviews and Feedback

Without an adequate number of positive reviews from guests a holiday rental lacks credibility. But today even popular holiday rentals struggle to get guest reviews. Today's guests have busy, time-poor lives. They are being assaulted on all sides by social media, advertising and overflowing email inboxes. Amidst this noise of the modern age holiday rental owners need to be prompted, reminded and even provided incentives for leaving reviews. Few holiday rental owners follow up with guests and ask them to review their property and even fewer have guest books at their properties. Whilst guest books may be seen as a little 'old school' they reinforce a positive customer experience when guests read them. Also, photos can be taken of guest book entries and used as marketing collateral.

Note: it's not acceptable (and in some countries illegal) to bribe guests to leave positive reviews!

Aside from gaining positive reviews to boost the property, guest feedback is critical to improving. Guests should always be given the opportunity to provide feedback. A good way to obtain guest feedback, but to focus on what's important is to email your database of guests an annual improvement survey (using an online survey tool such as Survey Monkey). This can also be used as a marketing tool to encourage future bookings by providing the guest with a discount voucher for their next stay upon completion of the survey. The important thing is that you act upon the feedback you receive!

Note: check the laws regarding email in your jurisdiction. It may be illegal for you to market to an email address that is provided by the booking websites.

Poor Maintenance and Cleanliness

If a guest's first impression of your property is a lack of cleanliness, no matter how good your property may be, it is a difficult hurdle to overcome. Guests don't want to arrive at a property and suddenly be made aware of previous guests. Hair in showers, stained carpets, dog hair on floors and smelly bed linen are just some of the factors that may have your guests running for the door or worse, leaving a negative review. There is no margin for error when it comes to cleanliness.

These issues can be overcome by carefully selecting your cleaning staff and by having quality standards checklists in place. And never, ever ask your guests to clean the property in place of professional cleaners.

A guest says ...

We enquired about a property and the owner responded and said that we could clean the property ourselves when we left for a reduced fee. We were aghast! Not only did we not want to clean a house on holiday, but we didn't feel that guests were capable of cleaning a property to the standard of professional cleaners. We imagined turning up at the property to find it had been cleaned poorly by guests and that was enough to put us off staying there.

Listing Your Property Online

The following sections explain the steps required to list your holiday rental on the booking websites (sometimes called OTAs – Online Travel Agencies).

Whilst there are differences between the booking websites there are a number of principles that you should always look to meet no matter the website. Consider these the Eight commandments of holiday rental websites. These are:

1. Always have high resolution professional photos
2. Write accurate, experience-based descriptions
3. Never cancel or decline bookings (unless guests have breached your rules)
4. Always have your booking calendar up-to-date (iCal sync)
5. Be ultra fast in responding to bookings
6. Always have pricing up-to-date
7. Concisely articulate your rules
8. Complete every available section of the booking website listing.

Photos

Without a shadow of a doubt, professionally-taken photos are the most important feature of a quality holiday rental listing. They will set you apart from the competition instantly, as long as your property has been set up according to the guidelines mentioned in Part 2 – i.e. clean and simple with no clutter.

Here are some of the things that will make guests switch off instantly:

- Fuzzy photos
- Dark photos; e.g. rooms with curtains or blinds closed
- Messy rooms, clutter, unmade beds
- Photos taken at 'artistic' angles
- Stretched photos; e.g. photos taken in portrait stretched to landscape.

Be wary of friends with fancy cameras masquerading as photographers! It almost always ends in disappointment.

Here's what's important to aim for:

- Photos are taken by a professional photographer experienced in real estate photography (ask for prior samples and references)
- The photographer can enhance the photos for you using Photoshop
- Photos of both inside and outside are part of the package
- Ensure photos are taken of every room
- Aim for a minimum of 20 photos
- Photos must be high resolution (at least 1Mb and not more than 20Mb)
- Photos are taken on a clear day with good natural light

- Shots of the front of the house should be in sun, not shade

- Photos are taken at a time of day when the property is shown in its best light (literally). At dusk, turn on all the lights inside and outside, and try to get a moody look. Use a tripod. It might take a few goes to get the balance just right.

- 2–3 location shots should also be provided.

If you are in any doubt as to the impact that professional photography can have, look at the photos of Sunbaker Beach House – *Before* (iPhone) and *After* (professional photography).

Before

After

Some websites now allow individual photos to be linked to specific rooms or to tag rooms with labels. For example, you can link a photo of a bunk bed bedroom to the bedroom listed as 'Bedroom 1 – Bunk Bed Room' to provide extra clarity to guests. This is something you should always do.

Another useful feature is the ability to add captions describing each photo. This is an opportunity not for a boring list of features but to capture the experience or additional features. Rather than 'Bunk Bed Room', write 'Two bunk beds that both adults and kids can sleep in in comfort'.

Drones

If you have a property that is close to a major attraction (think beach, bay, mountains or tourist attraction) then getting some drone shots done is a great idea. By positioning the drone showing your property and the distance to the attraction you can showcase its amazing position. If you have property on a large parcel of land, drone shots can also be an effective way of displaying the scale that standard photos cannot. Many drone operators can also take video for you. There's nothing quite as jaw dropping as a drone swooping over your property to reveal a spectacular vista.

Photo Order

The order of your photos is also critical. If your first few photos do not hit the spot in terms of what the guests want to see they will navigate away from your listing.

As a rough guide your photo order should follow this formula:

Photo One – Hero shot

The hero shot is incredibly important as it's often the only photo shown to guests in a long list of available properties. The hero shot should be the most attractive photo of the property – the photo with the 'wow factor' to make the guest want to see more. If you are lucky enough to have a stunning view or a unique feature (think swimming pools, spas and roaring fires) you should lead with that picture. If your property exterior is particularly impressive this can also make a good hero shot.

If your property isn't flashy, don't panic. Pick a nice outdoor area or cosy living room. If you get stuck, ask a few friends which photo would make them want to see more.

You may wish to alter your hero shot to cater for different times of year – for example, a roaring fire in winter and outdoor dining in summer.

You should never select a location shot, bathroom or laundry as a hero shot. Bedrooms also do not make great hero shots.

Photos Two to Six – Best of the Rest

The next photos should include the following areas:

- Living area
- Outdoor entertaining area/pool
- Dining area
- One bedroom (best one)
- Kitchen

The rest of your photos should include any other areas that have not yet been displayed:

- Additional living areas
- Other bedrooms
- Bathrooms
- Laundry
- Gardens/grounds
- Property exterior

If you have multiple photos of the same rooms think carefully as to whether they add value to the listing. If they don't, do not include them. If they do add value, place them in your listing after the photos above.

Lastly, add a couple of location shots to give context to your listing's location.

Floor Plans

Floor plans are a convenient way for guests to understand the layout of your property and can usually be done by the professional photographer taking your photos. Floor plans should show the full property layout (including garden if possible), doors, windows and key fixtures and fittings such as kitchen benches, tables, chairs, wardrobes and beds.

Don't just go for a black and white real estate style floor plan. Floor plans today can be done in a 3D style with amazing attention to detail such as the one below:

Virtual Tours

Virtual allow guests to 'move' through the interior of the property (a bit like Google Street View does with maps) and they are becoming more popular. Currently none of the main booking websites permit the upload of virtual tours, but it will change in the near future. It is, however, possible to add these to your own website.

Video

Very few holiday rentals use video to promote their properties and it is a massive missed opportunity. The growth of video as a marketing mechanism is huge and is ideally suited to a holiday rental property. With YouTube now the second most used search engine in the world, having a property video can be a fantastic competitive advantage. Booking websites are now starting to offer the ability to add videos (so long as you don't include links to your website, a competitor website or include any way for the guest to contact you directly) and videos can also be added to your own website very easily if you decide to go down that path.

Most professional photographers will also be able to take video for you. You can either get them to edit the video for you or you can hire someone to do it for you. If you choose to hire someone to edit it here's what you'll need to do:

Upload all of the files to a cloud-based storage provider, such as Google Drive or Dropbox. Both of these provide free plans that you can use temporarily if you don't want to use the service on an ongoing basis.

Post a job on upwork.com, freelancer.com or a similar website where you can obtain skilled virtual workers to edit your video. Be sure to ask for samples of their work. As a rough guide you will pay $50–100 (fixed price) to edit your footage into a one to two minute video (make sure your video is not any longer than two minutes).

Be sure to create written captions that outline the key features of each room. Ideally add any logos, awards and most importantly your website URL for bookings.

Note: have two versions of the video created: one without contact details to use with the booking websites and another with contact details to use on your website and on YouTube. Currently only HomeAway permits the upload of a property video.

If you are having difficulty describing what you want, you can use the following template:

Job: Edit Video to Create two-minute Video for Holiday Rental Property

I am looking for someone to edit and produce a highly professional two-minute video from video taken of my holiday rental property. Details of the property are available at <insert a link to your property>. Video files created must be suitable for upload to YouTube.

Make sure you specify a timeframe for completion.

Once you are happy with the completed video, upload it to the booking websites that accept videos, YouTube, your website and social media.

Property Description

The next most important factor to get right (photos being the first) is the description of your property. If you think of your photos as the cake, the description is the icing!

Property Title

The property title is not just for the name of your property – it's an opportunity to sell the best features of it. For example:

Hayes Beach House – Pet-friendly Award Winner – 4 Mins Walk to Beach

The title clearly shows the name but also includes the fact that the property has won an award and is very close to the beach. It is better to describe the distance to attractions in terms of minutes walk rather than the distance in metres. For some reason 250 metres sounds like a longer walk than 4 minutes – but they are exactly the same!

The challenge with the property description is to describe the experience your guests are looking for. It should not be a list of facts about what your property does and doesn't have – the websites have this covered in their settings.

Different booking websites have different property title lengths available, so you'll have to play around to find out what works best. If you have a long property name – Hayes Beach House, for example – consider shortening it to Hayes@Callala and save space for the unique selling points.

Snapshot

Your first paragraph should be captivating enough to have the guest wanting to know more. For example:

Imagine being only four minutes walk from sinking your toes into the world famous pure white sands of Jervis Bay. Where you can float under blue skies in water as crystal clear as a mountain stream. Where your four-legged friend can run for kilometres and the kids can play in the water without care whilst mum and dad relax. And when you return home exhilarated and refreshed there's a hot outdoor shower to wash the sand from between your toes.

Note the inclusion of words that create emotional connections with the guest: sinking, floating, relax, exhilarated, refreshed! Most owners miss the mark completely as they are focussing on the features of the property and as a result they all sound the same (and none of them sounds unique).

The trick with property descriptions is to showcase your features from an experiential point of view. Rather than say you have a BBQ on the back deck, describe the coming together of family around a meal. Rather than saying you have a big hammock, describe the *experience* of relaxing in the hammock looking at the stars.

If you feel that you don't have the skills to create a compelling description, don't worry. It is worth investing in having your description professionally written. Online services such as Guesthook (https://guesthook.com/) will do it all for you for a fee.

For example:

You'll be staying at an award-winning, pet-friendly house where every comfort and convenience has been provided. Brushed with a beautiful, classic beach house style with light-filled interiors maybe you'll sip a cool drink in the sunroom's hammock chairs whilst listening to the waves crash in the distance or enjoy a wine on the back deck whilst the cockatoos circle and squawk.

The family-sized hammock on the deck is the ideal spot to launch a tennis ball to the dog, read a book from the library or watch the children play with the toys in the fully secure garden. Or maybe you'll just keep it to yourself whilst you watch the sunset turn to the most magnificent display of the Milky Way you've ever seen.

When you do come inside your only difficulty will be deciding how to relax. Maybe kick back on the couch and enjoy a DVD or Foxtel on the big screen TV – or pick one of the 10,000 songs on the iPod stereo – or reconnect the family over a well-contested game of Monopoly or Scrabble. Whilst the kids and dog play with the toys you can be busy uploading your amazing holiday photos using the complimentary unlimited Wi-Fi.

On the deck the family chef can show off their culinary skills on the 4-burner BBQ before everyone gathers around the big outdoor table to laugh, tell tales and enjoy a memorable feast. In the cooler months former boy scouts will delight in filling the house with a toasty glow from the combustion fire.

When it's finally time to hit the hay, you'll find three bedrooms all with inviting queen and single beds, two warm showers, extra pillows and blankets if you need them and plenty of storage for all your things. Fans for summer and heaters for winter will keep you so comfortable that you won't want to get up the next day. But you'll already know from our exclusive guidebook that there are so many things to see and do in the Jervis Bay area – from where to shop and where to dine out to in-the-know local knowledge of the area's hidden secrets that you'll want to jump out of bed and explore!

But before you head out for the day be sure to enjoy a lazy holiday breakfast on the back deck or at the breakfast bar where the barista of the family can test their cappuccino-making skills on the top of the range Sunbeam dual boiler espresso machine.

Holidays are precious and memories are forever. We invite you to make beautiful family memories with us at Hayes Beach House.

Who Are You?

Each booking website allows the entry of information about who you are. This is a good opportunity to build trust with the guest and to explain why you bought your property and why you love the area so much. Do not underestimate the power of a well-written bio that conveys your passion for the unique aspects of the area.

For example, tell your guests about your family and pets (particularly if you are pet friendly), tell them about the things that you like to do in the area, your favourite restaurants or even that magic spot at the house where you love to relax.

Property Facilities

Whilst the property description is about experience and emotion, the booking websites will require you to complete factual information about the property. It is critically important that you complete every field possible within the booking websites. Be careful that you do not miss options. There are many specific settings within the booking websites that are not easy to find at first glance. Go through every possible menu and every screen one by one and complete every field.

What Is Provided?

It's a good idea to clearly state upfront what you *do* and *don't* provide in order to avoid disappointment when guests arrive. It also helps guests prepare adequately so that they can enjoy the property better when they arrive. This is also a good opportunity to describe any optional extras that guests may want to add to their booking. Some of the booking websites will provide options to select these (such as linen or pet friendly) but if there is something specific that guests need to know be sure to include it in your description or house rules.

A guest says ...

We rented a magnificent waterfront property. It was advertised as a family-friendly holiday house. Our expectation was that there would be at least a few board games and some toys. Sadly, there was neither, and we said so on the review.

Rules

Rules are a very important part of your property information not only because they will stop guests booking that you don't want to stay but they also will allow you to cancel the booking without penalty .

For example:

- *Maximum six adults in any group of guests*
- *No bucks or hens groups*
- *Pets welcome but not on beds and couch please.*

Bear in mind that the more rules you have the more draconian you will appear to guests. Guests don't want to stay in properties with onerous levels of rules. Any more than 3–4 rules and you risk putting guests off staying there.

A guest says ...

We were looking at booking a holiday rental and noticed a huge list of rules that the owner had included, one of which was 'No eating in bed'. It put us off booking as we wanted to relax on holiday, not be worried about doing something wrong.

You should also avoid the use of signs at your property as this creates a very inhospitable atmosphere. One or two signs detailing house rules or important information (preferably enclosed within cupboards) is enough.

Documenting Your Description

It is a very good idea to document your property description in a separate document (e.g. MS Word/Google Docs) so that you can copy and paste it into the different property websites you'll be listing on.

Pricing

Getting your pricing right is one of the most critical elements of a successful holiday rental property. Unfortunately, it's the most common area owners make mistakes with. Both underpricing and overpricing are common problems. The following section will discuss how you can set pricing that hits the sweet spot of your customers. But first let's look at some of the most common mistakes of pricing.

One Price Fits All

Wherever you may be in the world you will be affected by varying demand at different times of year. Holiday periods in both hemispheres, weekends and weekdays, special events all have an impact on pricing. So if pricing is set at the same rate all the time it's showing a lack of understanding of customer demand. Prices may be too high in the off season and too low in the high season, and special events will represent a missed opportunity altogether.

From a customer perspective, seeing one rate for the entire year does not instil confidence. In fact, it creates doubt as to the professionalism of the owner. A customer looking to immediately book for a specific price for specific dates may simply move onto a competitor as they fear that if they enquire they will be sent back a different rate from the one quoted on the website (and typically they will be correct). This creates a great deal of frustration for customers who simply want to pay the price they see on the website.

Never Changing Pricing

There are some holiday rental owners who set pricing once and never change it again. This is madness! Pricing should be continuously improved based on market conditions and reviewed every month to ensure that enquiry and conversion rates are hitting appropriate targets. Some owners try to maintain pricing so that they can encourage repeat business for the same guests. Your holiday rental is not a charity and if guests do not want to pay the appropriate market rate there are others that will!

An owner says ...

We bought an existing holiday rental where the owner had been charging the same rate over Christmas for several years as she had loyal customers. It was no surprise they were loyal as the price was $1,000 below the weekly market rate! When we took over we raised the price by $1,000 much to the shock of the loyal customers who were used to receiving a bargain price. We lost all of those customers but we still booked out every week during that period at the higher rate, increasing our revenue by $6,000 in one month.

Selling a Secret

No matter how appropriately priced your accommodation is, if people can't find your property on booking websites or via web searches, you are wasting your time. Holiday rental owners frequently fall into a downward spiral of price reduction by assuming that because they aren't getting bookings their price is too high. The simplest way of understanding whether the price is too high is to calculate your conversion rate (% of enquiries converting to bookings). If your conversion rate is low (below 15%) and you are doing everything else right (professional photos, fast response times, easily visible on a range of booking websites) then it is likely that your price is too high. If the conversion rate is good (above 20%) but you are staring at an empty calendar then the chances are that your problem is not one of pricing but that your enquiry rate is too low. That is, you are selling a secret – a property that is not high enough in search rankings to be visible to potential guests. Conversely, if you are experiencing extremely high rates of conversion (e.g. above 50%) your property is likely to be underpriced.

Setting Pricing

Setting your pricing for the first time can be a daunting experience. The following sections will detail ways of setting your pricing so that you are neither under- nor over-charging for your property.

If there is one principle with pricing above all others it's that the guest should always pay the amount they are quoted on the website. Trying to add extra fees after booking is not only a poor experience but can lead to your property being banned from the booking website. Of course if a guest wishes to modify a booking and this results in an extra charge that is perfectly acceptable.

Structuring Your Pricing

Owners often start out with a nightly rate that includes cleaning. Here's why this is not a good idea.

Having cleaning included in your rate might sound like a simpler option but it becomes problematic with shorter stays. As the stay duration decreases the overall profitability declines.

For example, a $200 booking for one night with a $150 cleaning fee provides a profit of $50. Whilst a $400 booking for two nights has a profit of $250. As a result many owners think that 1 night bookings are not worth the effort – and they are right if they are including the cleaning fee in the rate.

But because there are many guests looking for one night stays, and there isn't as much availability, guests are prepared to pay more. So rather than setting an all-inclusive rate of $200 a night, it pays to split the nightly rate into two components:

1. Base Rate
2. Cleaning Fee.

For example, you set your base rate at $100 and your cleaning fee at $150. The total cost to the guest is $250 and you make enough for it to be worthwhile. What's more the property becomes available to a bigger market and increases its chances of being booked.

With the cleaning fee separated your bookings are always profitable, no matter how short the duration.

You may also want to consider adding a linen fee per person to cover additional costs if your cleaners charge you for the linen on a per bed basis – just be sure to look at the total price to ensure it is competitive in the marketplace.

An owner says ...

Our competitors are stuck in the dark ages. They set a minimum 7-night stay period for peak seasons and miss out on many bookings because there are so many guests now looking for shorter stays.

Analysing the Competition

The great thing about the online world is that every piece of pricing for your competitors is on display for you to access – as is their availability calendar (and if they don't have a calendar they are not worth looking at).

This information can be used to provide a simple pricing guideline prior to listing your property for rental. The key variables for pricing relate to the number of guests you can host, quality of the accommodation

109

and distance to the key attractions. Try to pick out those properties that have the highest amount of bookings in their calendar.

Example:

Property Name	Guest Capacity	Proximity to Attractions	Quality	Rate - Low Season (weekday)	Rate - Low Season (weekend)	Rate - Peak Season (midweek)	Rate - Peak Season (weekend)	Average $ Per Guest
Sea Breeze Apartment	6	Medium	Medium	$230	$320	$440	$440	$59.58
Magic Lookout	13	Medium	High	$775	$800	$840	$800	$61.83
Beached Whale	12	Low	Medium	$245	$340	$375	$940	$39.58
Star Lookout	16	Low	High	$710	$950	$855	$955	$54.22
Your Property	8	High	High	$245	$395	$600	$600	$57.50

Resist the temptation to price yourself below the competition to capture more customers if you believe your property is of higher quality. This can lead to your property being viewed as a budget property, when many customers want to rent higher quality properties in your area. Also, customers on a budget may not fully respect your property.

Varying Pricing

Properties should never have the same pricing all year round. It is also important to consider the minimum nightly stay for different periods throughout the year. Here are some common scenarios of when you may wish to increase or decrease pricing.

Weekends

If your property is close to a large population centre and is seen as an attractive weekend destination you can substantially increase weekend pricing.

Don't sell yourself short on weekend pricing. If demand is high don't offer 1-night stays and make sure that your rates for Saturday and Sunday night combined equal the same rate as Friday and Saturday night combined. Whilst Friday and Saturday night stays are more popular with weekenders, a proportion of guests prefer to stay Saturday and Sunday night. Don't miss out on a high weekend rate by dropping your Sunday night rate! As a rough guide, if you are within three hours of a major city your nightly weekend rate should be roughly double your midweek rate. If you find that weekend dates are booking out months in advance, raise the price.

An owner says ...

We charge $800 for a 2-night weekend stay. We can do this as we are two hours from a major city and demand is high. Midweek is less in demand as most of our target guests are working during the week so our midweek rates are 50% less than our weekend rates.

Weeknights

In popular holiday destinations where guests are more likely to spend a week or longer you may be best advised to set weekday pricing the same as your weekend pricing. If demand is high enough for weeklong stays you could specify a minimum 7-night stay. The advantage of this is that you can reduce your overall costs as opposed to shorter stays, as you are cleaning less often.

Weekly Rates

Weekly rates are often slightly discounted to encourage guests to book longer stays (thereby reducing cleaning costs if you have an all-inclusive rate). As a ballpark, a 5–10% discount is not uncommon. If you have periods of the year that are heavily in demand you should not provide any discount at all (and charge several times your peak rate).

Seasonal Pricing

The majority of properties will set pricing based on different seasons. This doesn't necessarily mean that you will need to set different prices for all four seasons, but it's likely that demand will vary at least between summer and winter. Think carefully about how seasonality may affect demand for your property.

For example:

- Beach houses will experience high demand in summer
- Mountain properties in ski areas will experience higher demand in winter.

It's also important to remember that in some parts of the world summer is too hot and winter is too cold!

A guest says ...

We booked a property, only to find out when we got there that it was the rainy season. We spent a week at the apartment staring out the window at torrential rain but we didn't mind as we'd gotten a week away in a lovely property at a great price!

Holiday Periods (long weekends, school holidays)

Holiday periods (such as school, university and public holidays) can be a boon for holiday rental properties. Prior to setting up your pricing you should identify all the public holidays and other significant school holidays in your area and vary your pricing accordingly. Public holidays falling on a Monday or Friday are typically in demand as they allow guests to have a long weekend without taking time off work. You should also look to set minimum 3-night stays for long weekends. For example, for a public holiday falling on a Monday, set a minimum 3-night stay for Friday, Saturday and Sunday, all at a higher rate. This prevents underselling the weekend by only recouping a 2-night sale.

An owner says ...

Our Easter Long Weekend nightly rate is our most expensive of the entire year at more than five times our midweek off-peak rate. We also specify a 3-night minimum stay so as to maximise revenue.

Special Events

Be sure to research special events in your area by speaking to locals (in person or on local Facebook groups), tourist information centres and other businesses in the area. These can cause large spikes of visitor numbers and you can raise your prices significantly due to high demand; for example, festivals or sporting events.

Last Minute Discounts

Last minute discounts can be a good way to fill up spare capacity that is unlikely to sell. Many holiday rental owners fail to offer these discounts and miss a significant opportunity. Some booking websites allow guests to filter by discount or special deal and prominently display the discounts, thereby attracting further attention. Discounts can typically be set as a percentage rate for a specified period in advance. A 20% discount for bookings within the next seven days is a substantial enough discount (for a property accessible within three hours of a capital city) that will help to fill up spare capacity. If your property is further afield (for example requires a plane flight to get to) you may wish to extend the window to 14 or even 30 days out.

An owner says ...

Be sure to work out the profit you make on the booking after cleaning fees and utility costs to make sure that you are still making enough money off the booking after applying the last minute discount.

Booking Window

All of the booking websites will ask you to select how far in advance guests can book. This is called the booking window. It is advisable to set a booking window of 12 months. Guests may wish to book far ahead for in-demand periods. If you are unsure whether you have got your pricing right for in-demand periods you may wish to set a shorter window until you gain confidence in your pricing.

For example, say you are not sure that your Christmas pricing is high enough – set your booking window to six months and wait until the end of the Christmas period and assess your occupancy. This will prevent guests from jumping in and booking a bargain rate for next year if you have set your prices too low. Once you are confident with your pricing you can then set the booking window to 12 months. However it is good practice to keep your pricing up-to-date for 18 months in advance so that you are not caught out.

Base Price

When setting up your listing on a booking website it will ask you for a base price. Be very careful with this price as it will set all dates to this price until you have updated your pricing with your seasonal and other rates. As a result, you should set this base price equal to your highest rate in the year. This way if you forget to update your pricing you won't have guests booking at a potentially lower rate.

Bond (security deposit)

A bond is an amount of money held either by the booking website or the owner which can be used to deduct extra fees from the guest such as charges for extra cleaning or damages. Some of the booking websites refer to it as a security deposit.

Not all owners choose to charge guests a bond. Damage to properties is rare but having a bond does definitely encourage good behaviour. The amount you decide to charge for a bond should be enough to make people think twice about getting up to any mischief! The bond amount will be the same for each group of guests and should be set at a reasonable level that is in line with the pricing of the property.

As a rough guide, take your lowest nightly weeknight price, double it then round it up or down to the nearest $100 and set your bond at this amount.

An owner says ...

We own a large property and frequently have large groups of guests staying with us for bucks or hens nights. As a result we charge a bond of $1,000 which ensures that they are on their best behaviour!

Minimum Stay Periods

The shorter your minimum stay period the greater are your opportunities to get bookings.

Deposit

All of the booking websites allow owners to set a deposit amount that the guest has to secure the booking. You should always charge a deposit for a booking and never, ever confirm a booking with a guest until they have paid it. Whilst some of the booking websites may try to convince you to not charge anything upfront, this is a foolhardy option that will lead to a slew of cancelled bookings and wasted time.

A 50% deposit, payable to confirm the booking with remaining 50% payable 30 days prior is quite acceptable. It's also a good customer service gesture to offer a period of free cancellation, but this should be a substantial period of time from the booking date – for example, 12 weeks out – in order to give you plenty of time to secure another booking.

Some websites have ridiculously weak cancellation policies allowing guests to cancel without penalty a few days from check-in. These policies should be avoided where possible.

Documenting Your Pricing

Documenting your pricing (e.g. in a spreadsheet) is an excellent idea as you can create formulas and play around with percentage discounts to understand profit margins.

Having different pricing for each website creates a level of complexity that can be challenging to keep track of. We recommend keeping pricing consistent across all booking websites.

Here's an example of how you might document your pricing:

	Sun	Mon	Tue	Wed	Thu	Fri	Sat	Fri+Sat	7 Nights	Min Stay
Winter	$215	$215	$215	$215	$215	$355	$355	$710	$1685	2 nights
May 27 - 31, June 2 - Sept 22, May 1 - June 8, Jun 12 - Sep 28										
Summer	$255	$255	$255	$255	$255	$410	$410	$820	$1995	2 nights
Sep 23 - Dec 19, Jan 27 - Apr 13, Apr 17-30										
Long Wknds Summer	$600					$600	$600	$1800		3 nights
Sep 29 - Oct 1										
Xmas / New Year	$650	$650	$650	$650	$650	$650	$650	$1300	$4550	2 nights
Dec 23 - Jan 7										
Xmas / Jan School Holiday	$600	$600	$600	$600	$600	$600	$600	$1200	$4200	2 nights
Dec 20 - Dec 22, Jan 8 - Jan 26										
Long Weekend	$500					$500	$500	$1500		3 nights
Jun 9 - Jun 11										
Easter Weekend	$900					$900	$900	$2400		3 nights

Be sure to add your applicable dates in for each rate. The documented pricing can then be used as a reference guide that you can quickly use to check rates without having to log into systems.

An owner says ...

Don't be afraid to be the most expensive property if yours is the best! We are the most expensive in our area but we get the most bookings and make the most money because our facilities and location are superior to all other properties in the area.

Dynamic Pricing

For the more tech-savvy hosts, dynamic pricing software is worth investigating. Dynamic pricing software allows hosts to automatically update their pricing based on market demand. The software uses booking data from your property's area to automatically increase or decrease your price. Hosts can set minimum and maximum prices and then let the software do the rest. The software can also look at the property's occupancy over time and modify the price accordingly.

Dynamic pricing is not to be confused with Airbnb's Smart Pricing. Smart Pricing should be avoided at all costs as it recommends extremely low rates in order to get properties fully occupied quickly.

Guest Guidebook

Once you have your listing set up with photos, descriptions and pricing it's time to create your Guest Guidebook. A Guest Guidebook details not just everything the guest needs to know about the property, but also includes details of amenities and attractions in the surrounding area. Sadly many property owners neglect this very important part of the booking process and create extra work for themselves having to field a multitude of questions from impending guests. A great Guest Guidebook can not only eliminate extra work for the host, but can significantly add to the guest's experience. It sets up the stay in the best manner possible and sets a professional tone for the rest of their experience. A guide can be the difference between a good or a great review if done properly.

Long text-based emails, Word documents and PDF files are the domain of amateurish owners. Today owners should always invest in an online guidebook system such as Hostfully (www.hostfully.com). Online guidebooks take the guest experience to a new level. Some of their features include:

- Optimised display for different devices (mobile, desktop)
- Map-based view that links to Google maps for easy navigation
- Ability to print a paper version (if required).

A guest says ...

We like to sit down and plan our holiday before we get there, so it is a frustrating experience when the owners provide details on how to get into the property and nothing else. We have wasted a lot of time trying to figure out where to find a good place to have dinner or the best attractions to visit. The best holiday rentals take the effort out of these things by providing all the details upfront so we can plan prior to arrival.

Here's a summary of what to include in your Guest Guidebook:

- How to get to the property (directions/map)
- Where to stop on the way
- How to access the property (keys/codes)
- Check-in/out times
- What is supplied
- What to bring

- Bedding details

- How to use appliances (TV/DVD, stereo, Wi-Fi, kitchen appliances, heating/cooling)

- House Rules

- Local attractions

- Where to eat out (cafes/restaurants/take aways)

- Where to buy food/drink

- Owner contact information

- Emergency contact information

- Check-out process

- Things to see and do.

You should only send your guidebook to the guest upon confirmation of the booking. And you should only confirm a booking when payment has been confirmed. Sending the Guest Guidebook as early as possible helps guests to 'self serve' and find answers to their own questions so they don't need to ask you!

Whilst most guests will access the online version it's also a good idea to have a printed and laminated copy at the property for those guests that are not tech savvy.

Frequently Asked Questions (FAQs)

As a holiday rental owner you will find that guests will frequently ask the same questions prior to their stay. In order to avoid having to answer the same questions over and over again it's worthwhile to create a frequently asked question and answer list. These can be used to create templates within the booking websites or simply kept handy so that you can cut and paste responses. It's also a good idea to include these FAQs with your response to enquiries. As a starting point some common questions are likely to be:

- What is the bedding configuration?
- What is your maximum occupancy?
- Are you pet friendly?
- How close is the <popular attraction>?
- Are there any restaurants or cafes nearby?
- Are there shops nearby? (particularly food/drink)
- Do you have Wi-Fi?
- How do I access the property?
- Is there parking at the property?
- What payment methods do you accept?
- Do you have a portacot or high chair available?

Creating a document with FAQs and answers and saving on a cloud drive (e.g. Google Drive/Dropbox) means that you can quickly and easily copy text into your response.

The benefit to having prepared FAQs is that the quicker you can answer guest questions the less likely that the guest will shop around looking at other properties. The easier it is for the guest to get the information they need, the greater the chance of the guest booking with you. By providing this level of professionalism it also sets the tone for what the experience will be when the guest stays at the property.

If your phone number is listed on websites (for example Google My Business) you will get the occasional phone call from guests – but if your property is located in a high demand area you can expect a deluge of calls from the last-minute brigade every long weekend. This can be a huge time waster.

The best course of action in this situation is to develop a standard text that you can send to anyone that calls you, as follows:

Hi, thanks for your enquiry for <property name>. To view availability and book online instantly, please visit our website at <URL>.

Simply divert calls to voicemail then text the guest.

You'll find that 95% will visit the website, see that their dates aren't available or the price is too high for them and move on.

Terms and Conditions

It only takes one customer complaint to realise that you need a solid set of terms and conditions to protect yourself and your property.

For an individual property owner these terms and conditions do not need to be onerous and should cover the following:

- Cancellation or modifications to bookings
- House Rules (activities not allowed, pets, etc.)
- Maximum number of guests
- Check-in/out times (including late check-out policy)
- Check-out instructions
- Additional fees (excess cleaning, damage, noise, etc.)
- Liability statement (no liability for guest loss, etc.)

You do not need to specify payment rules that are covered by the booking website.

Some websites allow the upload of a set of terms and conditions that are displayed during the booking process. If this isn't available, send a copy to the guest as part of the booking confirmation or include them in your Guest Guidebook. If you don't display all of them on the booking website you must make it clear in the house rules section of the booking website that they will be required to accept additional terms and conditions.

Cancellations

Many guests think that booking a holiday rental is like booking a hotel room. They don't understand that by cancelling a booking (particularly at the last minute) that a holiday rental owner has a limited opportunity of re-booking the property.

Guests will often try to play on the heartstrings with excuses as to why they had to cancel in an attempt to get their fees refunded. You are running a business and should stick to only refunding according to the policy of the website booked through.

As a result, it is also a good idea to recommend to guests that they purchase travel insurance in the event that they need to cancel, even if only to say to guests 'well we told you so' when they kick up a fuss when you inform them they won't get their money back after cancelling!

Some booking websites can, unfortunately, overrule your terms and conditions and refund guests if they believe that there are genuine extenuating circumstances such as illness.

Websites to List On

Once you have your descriptions documented and your photos and pricing ready it's time to list your property for rental online. There are a multitude of holiday rental websites out there and they all have different pricing structures. There are two main pricing methods adopted by these websites:

Pay-per-booking

Over the past few years all of the major holiday rental websites have moved to success-based pricing models, otherwise known as 'pay per booking'.

This payment model has become the default in the industry as there is no upfront fee and therefore no financial risk for the owner. In this model the owner pays a % fee when the guest books. Some websites (such as Airbnb and HomeAway) also charge the guest a % service fee in addition to the owner fee. As a result, these websites have high numbers of listings and therefore provide a great deal of choice for guests. Owner fees typically range from 3–15% of the total booking amount.

Some owners are put off listing on certain booking websites because of the fees they charge. This is a big mistake that inexperienced owners make. The most important thing is to get bookings irrespective of the fees charged by the website. If your property becomes fully booked then by all means reduce the number of websites you are listed on to save fees; but until then take the bookings irrespective of the fees.

Upfront Payment

This involves the property owner paying an upfront fee (typically annually) and may be split into gold/silver/bronze style packages where the property receives more exposure to customers the higher the price paid.

Annual listings requiring upfront payments are rarely good value. Guests will typically gravitate to websites that have the biggest selection of properties and those that charge upfront fees don't have as large a selection. This is because owners are nervous about listing with them due to their unknown returns.

Owners should also be wary of new websites popping up and announcing themselves with great fanfare. Often these are scam websites set up in other countries where they have copied listings from bona fide websites to make their websites look established. They will often send spam email with special sign-up offers. They typically disappear a couple of months later (disappearing with everyone's money too). A good way to spot a scam website is to check their About pages (to see if they have a management team) or to Google the website to identify anything that does not look legitimate.

So what websites should you be listing your property on?

123

The Big Three

There are a number of major players in the global holiday rental industry and you should certainly list on not one, but all of them. Why? In different areas of countries and indeed different areas of the world there is varying uptake by guests (and in some countries they play second fiddle to locally based websites). With all of these websites offering a pay-per-booking service there is no harm in listing on all of them – this way you can try them out and then measure which are effective for you.

It is also critically important that you spread the risk and are not listed on only one booking website. In other words, never have all your eggs in one basket.

An owner says ...

During the Coronavirus pandemic Airbnb decided to refund guests in full without our consent. HomeAway and Booking.com left the refunds at our discretion. If we had only been on Airbnb our bookings would have been reduced to almost nothing.

The following is a summary of the Big Three websites that operate globally:

Website Name	Summary
Airbnb	The poster boy of the holiday rental industry Airbnb has grown rapidly to become one of the biggest holiday rental firms in the world. Key to its success is the ability to rent out not just an entire home but single rooms. Despite opposition from apartment residents and hotel chains, Airbnb continues to grow. It has a strong presence throughout the world, particularly in major capital cities. It appeals strongly to international travellers, couples and those on a budget, but its appeal is becoming more mainstream as time progresses with the term 'an airbnb' being synonymous with short-term rentals.
HomeAway	HomeAway is the second biggest globally and has acquired a number of holiday rental firms internationally over the last ten years (notably VRBO in the US and Stayz in Australia). Traditionally HomeAway has been a key player in the family and group market but is stepping up its focus in major cities in order to compete with Airbnb.
Booking.com	This is the new kid on the block, growing at a fast pace. It has already established itself as one of the major players in the holiday rental industry globally.

All of the major websites have functionality that will allow calendars to sync so that you don't have to enter the same booking into multiple systems (e.g. Airbnb syncs with HomeAway and Booking.com and vice versa).

National-based Websites

Whilst the Big Three may bring you guests from around the globe, it doesn't always mean that they will be the most effective. You may find that there are websites that are based solely within your country that will bring you more bookings.

There is no harm signing up for a few national websites to test them out (presuming they are on a pay-per-booking model). If you find that they are not providing you with bookings you can always de-list from them.

An owner says ...

If you decide that a particular website is not bringing you adequate returns make sure you request that your property is deleted from their website and *any partner websites they may be affiliated with. A year after delisting from a website we found our property appearing in Google search results as being available to book through that website. When the link was clicked it took them to a range of competitor properties. We contacted them immediately and requested that all details be deleted.*

Niche Websites

If you have a particular niche that your property appeals to you may wish to list with niche websites. For example, pet-friendly websites continue to grow in popularity.

Tourism Bodies

Tourism organisations can also be a useful option to advertise your property on and many have systems that you can list your property on for free and which will propagate details to multiple websites. Saying that, tourism websites still play second fiddle to the commercial operators and struggle to get anywhere near the same amount of web traffic. As they typically do not charge for listings they are still a worthwhile option. Some also integrate with booking software so that guests are taken to your website to book. If you don't have a website you may be able to provide a link to your listing on a commercial website such as HomeAway or Airbnb.

Property Managers

Prior to the advent of the Internet, real estate agents were the only option for holiday rental owners to list and book out their properties. Over the past ten years there has been a significant shift from the all-in-one real estate agent (selling and renting both long- and short-term) to the specialist short-term property manager. A specialist property manager can be an excellent option for those owners that are:

- Lacking time to manage a holiday rental (for example, the owners both work full-time)
- Not confident with technology
- Don't live near to the property and need on-site assistance.

When looking to use a property manager it's important to ask them a number of key questions and speak to some of their current owners to see how happy they are with their service:

1. How many properties do you manage?

If they are only managing between 1–5 properties it is likely they do not have the systems and processes in place to manage a portfolio of properties, but everyone has to start somewhere so if they are small ask what their roadmap is for development of their service. Smaller managers have less to lose so the business folding is a realistic possibility.

If they are managing 5–20 properties it's likely they've developed reasonable processes and systems and above 20 it would be almost impossible to manage a portfolio of properties without the required property management software ...

2. What property management system do you use?

The key response you are looking for here is that they actually do have one and it is a reputable system (check out capterra software reviews at https://www.capterra.com/). If they say that they use spreadsheets or 'just manage it within the booking websites', head for the hills.

3. What hours do your staff answer enquiries?

This is critically important and you should be looking for coverage seven days a week.

4. How fast do you respond to guest enquiries?

Ensure that they provide in writing that guest enquiries are responded to within two hours at the most.

5. Do you have staff that can attend in the event of an emergency?

They must have staff that can be at a property within thirty minutes in the event of an emergency or issue.

6. What fees do you charge the owner?

Typically this will be a % fee based on the booking value but many property managers charge significant extra (and unnecessary) fees such as property set-up fees and annual listing fees that can run into thousands of dollars. If your property manager charges up-front or annual fees, look elsewhere.

7. What fees do you charge the guest?

Many property managers charge the guest extra fees such as booking fees and damage protection fees. These are again unnecessary and are merely a means for the property manager to boost their profits. They also increase the price to the guest thereby potentially reducing bookings.

8. What is your average $ revenue per year per property?

Ask them to provide details of a range of properties in your area and the average revenue that they are achieving.

9. Are they a HomeAway Premier Partner or Airbnb Superhost?

Both of these programs display that high standards are being met but they can be difficult for property managers with a range of properties of different quality levels to achieve.

'Hotel Websites'

It's important to note that many of the websites that were previously the domain of hotels are now opening themselves up to accept holiday rental properties as customers. Websites such as Expedia and Booking.com will gladly sign up holiday rental properties. So should you list with them?

These websites can certainly bring extra bookings but you will have to accept that your property will be sold like a hotel room. You will not have the opportunity to vet guests or to decline a booking (at least not easily and not without penalty). Owners have also experienced inaccurate details being published on these websites due to the limitations of the systems. With these kinds of websites switching on to the burgeoning holiday rental market it is likely that this will not always be the case but it appears that there is some way to go before these websites are fully optimised for holiday rental owners.

The Cost versus Revenue Delusion

Many property owners fall into the trap of focusing on the fees that websites charge rather than the revenue that they bring in. The most important factors that you can use to assess the effectiveness of the website is the amount of bookings and revenue that they bring in. Fees are secondary. The only time you should be comparing website fees is when your property gets to the point where it is consistently booking out periods of the year. In this case you should review the booking websites you use in order to funnel traffic via your URL to the best option for you – or even better, your own website.

Your Own Website – Is It Worth It?

The vast majority of guests today will turn to holiday rental websites such as Airbnb as their first option when booking a holiday rental property, but this doesn't mean that you shouldn't have your own website. It also doesn't mean that you need to have it set up from day one. What is important to organise from the start is your own website URL and email address. Please don't use your personal email address to manage your properties – it looks unprofessional and your booking enquiries may get lost in a sea of your everyday emails.

A website URL (Uniform Resource Locator, often known as a domain name) is simply the website address that you will use. At Hayes Beach House the URL registered was www.hayesbeachhouse.com. When our company, Professional Holiday Homes was established we re-directed the URL to www.professionalholidayhomes.com (click to see what we mean).

You can register a website URL through many different domain name providers. Simply do a search on 'domain name registration' and you will find hundreds of providers. Prices of domain names vary slightly by provider but they are typically inexpensive and range from $10–$30 per year. Unless you intend to build a website you do not need to buy what is called 'hosting'. You may wish to check if domain name re-direction is included in the price as this is a very useful service if you decide not to build a website. Domain name re-direction allows you to send visitors from one URL to another. In the early days before our website was built the URL www.hayesbeachhouse.com was set to redirect to our HomeAway listing. This way potential guests from websites that didn't have book now functionality (such as tourism websites) could be funnelled towards a website where they could book. When the website with integrated online booking was in place the re-direction was switched off. This was a lot easier than going to every website and updating the URL.

Saying that, it is important to consider if a website is the right option for you. It's important to remember that your ranking on booking websites is usually driven by your performance on the website. Typically the more bookings and reviews you receive (and conversely the amount of requests you don't decline or cancel) will boost your rank so that your property appears higher in search results on the booking website. High rankings are critical for bookings.

An owner says ...

Analysis of our two properties revealed that there was a 400% difference in the number of listing views and booking enquiries between first and third place on a major website.

If you do decide that you want to build a website, the next section details the options for doing just that ...

Building a Website

There is a confusing array of options to build a website but there are two options to get you up and running quickly if you decide that building a website is what you want to do.

Option 1: The Self-build

There are a number of websites that offer templated websites that you can customise without the need for technical knowledge. Some of these websites (such as Wix.com or Logify.com) also have booking websites that seamlessly integrate with the website. Bear in mind that although these websites are relatively simple to operate it will still take several days for you to build a website on your own and may be beyond the ability level of those less technically savvy. An understanding of user experience design is also helpful.

Pros: Easy and cheap to set up, quick to build, no hosting fees

Cons: Ongoing monthly fees, lack of SEO (search engine optimisation) options

An owner says ...

We built our website using a Wix template and linked it to our website URL. Wix also had an integrated booking system (Wix hotels) that we found easy to set up and use. In total it took us three days to set up the website. However there was no facility to optimise our website for search engines and we were therefore unable to influence where we appeared in Google search results.

Option 2: Wordpress

Wordpress has become a very popular choice for anyone building a website. Wordpress is a step up in complexity from websites like Wix.com and requires a fair degree of technical understanding to get things the way you want them. A Google search will reveal a wide range of Wordpress templates suitable for holiday rental properties – some with booking systems. Due to the learning curve and time involved to set up you may wish to find someone skilled in Wordpress to build it for you. Bear in mind however, that there is always a large amount of to-ing and fro-ing with communication over website design which can take almost as much time as building it yourself!

If you do decide to hire someone to build the website for you, expect to pay anywhere from $500–$2000 depending on the features and pages you want. The cost will also vary depending upon where you source the freelancer from. Websites like upwork.com are a great source of freelancers but the quality varies considerably. Be sure to select freelancers with good reviews and be prepared for communication issues and delays if you choose someone who does not have English as their native language. Certainly, you can save costs by hiring someone from overseas but you'll have to weigh up whether it is worth it in the long run.

Pros: Flexible, fully featured, Advanced SEO

Cons: Complex, time-consuming, requires technical skills or outsourcing for a fee

Online Booking Systems

A critical part of your website is to have online booking – that is a guest can access a calendar to see available dates, select dates, pay and receive a confirmation email with all the required details automatically. If you build a website without a booking system you are doing your business more damage than good. If you have a website customers expect to be able to book through it, so if you don't have online booking they will be frustrated by the experience and will go elsewhere.

Many of the templates available through Wordpress or other website systems such as Wix, have booking systems but be aware that many were designed with hotels in mind, so be sure to try a few different options to find the one that suits your needs. In particular, if you charge a bond (otherwise known as a security deposit) you may find that many of the online booking systems do not have the functionality to charge and refund bonds.

An owner says ...

When we built our website we found that we had to set up our two properties as 'rooms' because the system was designed for hotels. This meant it couldn't cater for two different addresses and when it came to the automated confirmation email we had to send the instructions for both properties together as the system didn't have the functionality to send different emails for different 'room' types. This was not a great experience for guests who were confused by the two different sets of instructions.

Channel Management Software

If you have multiple properties or are listed with several different websites you may wish to investigate using channel management software. Channel management software is a system that talks to other websites and updates them so that you don't have to manually update details (prices, calendars) in each system. They can also integrate with your website to provide online booking functionality. The advantage of channel management software is that it can list your holiday rental on a large range of websites so that you can achieve more bookings.

In terms of disadvantages, channel management software can be hard to learn to use and because it must cater for a wide range of websites you may find them to be limited in functionality. They can also be expensive and may not include the ability to process payments.

Payment Gateways

Unless your website's booking system has an integrated payment system you will also require a payment gateway. This is a system that allows you to collect payments from your website or channel management software and to send them to your bank account. You may have heard of payment gateways such as Paypal or Stripe. Again you'll need to set these up so that they can integrate with your website or channel management software. Be sure to check which payment gateways are compatible before you go through the set-up process. Typically payment gateways charge a percentage of the fee the guest pays (usually 2–3% plus a small fee of a few cents per transaction).

An owner says ...

In an effort to reduce costs we decided to set up a website for our properties. We spent $1,000 having the website built, then had to pay 2.2% of revenue for the channel management software and 2.9% for the payment gateway. In total our fees per transaction were 5.1% – more than we were paying with some of our booking websites! We found the channel management software clunky, expensive and difficult for customers to book through.

Managing Enquiries and Bookings

The time will come when you're about to publish your property listing online and be ready to take bookings. This is an exciting time but you may be filled with a sense of 'have I thought of everything?' Before you press the button on publishing your online listing it's a good idea to run through the following checklist in order to dot every i and cross every t.

Furniture and appliances installed?	
Utilities (electricity, gas, water, phone/Wi-Fi) ready?	
Keyless entry or keys cut and accessible?	
Cleaner arranged?	
Linen and supplies ready (if required)?	
Lawns mowed?	
Property cleaned?	
Online listings complete?	

All good? Then let's look at handling your first enquiry ...

Responding to Guest Enquiries

Don't expect a flurry of phone calls and emails when you first list your property online (but do expect a few).

When you do get that first enquiry it's important to start the way you wish to continue – professionally and rapidly. You'll be looking to respond no later than 30 minutes after the guest contacts you. Don't be discouraged when guests don't book. If more than 20% of enquiries are converting to bookings you are doing well!

But before you respond to the booking request, carefully check the details of the enquiry.

Note: All of the major holiday rental websites have 'Instant Booking' functionality. Some still allow you to accept or decline the booking but some (e.g. Airbnb) do not allow you to cancel the booking without penalty unless the guests have breached your booking rules. If you have this functionality switched on, be clear on what the ramifications are if you need to cancel the booking for any reason. Cancellations can lead to significant declines in ranking. Reduced rank means reduced visibility of your property for guests.

Vetting Guests

Remember that you don't have to accept a group that wants to stay at your property if you are not comfortable with them, although it should be noted that you should not discriminate (e.g. gender, race or age).

Check the number of guests on the booking. Does it exceed your maximum capacity? If the number of adults and children is specified are there too many adults to comfortably sleep at your property? Often guests will look at a property without checking the details in full. If you don't think your guests will be comfortable contact them to clarify your bedding arrangements and size of property. Don't be greedy and try to squeeze too many in. This will simply result in negative reviews. Also having too many guests in a booking can lead to greater wear and tear.

An owner says ...

When we had large groups of adults there was often extra cleaning required and an increased level of wear and tear. We eventually decided to cap the number of adults at a level we were comfortable with and haven't had any problems since.

The amount of vetting you do of guests really depends on your tolerance to risk. Typically an appropriately sized bond and rental agreement will ensure respectful behaviour. If your target market is families with pets you are unlikely to have many issues. You are unlikely to need to vet bookings that are for families but you should vet groups with six or more adults to ensure they are not going to cause disturbance to neighbours. If you feel that guests are deceiving you (which does sometimes happen) you should conduct searches on Facebook, LinkedIn and Google to try to identify them. If they are a group of adults looking for a place to party, politely decline their enquiry.

If you have an enquiry that comes through as all adults it is a good idea to double check with them whether it is indeed all adults or whether it is a mixture of adults and kids. Sometimes when submitting an enquiry guests will simply select a number of adults as they mistakenly think they are selecting the number of guests. This happens surprisingly regularly.

If you are very risk averse or cater for large groups that can become boisterous you can ask the person booking the property to supply identification such as a drivers license or passport. This is simply a means to verify who they say they are and offers little protection against ill behaviour – although it may make the guest think twice given that you know where they live!

A copy of their credit card also isn't a perfect deterrent as they can attempt to get any extra charges refunded to them if they initiate a chargeback through their credit card company. The credit card provider will side with their customer nine times out of ten.

Templated Responses

Responding to customer enquiries with templated responses will help you to appear professional and will reassure the customer that they are dealing with a reputable operator that won't let them down.

Many systems will provide you with the ability to add and save your own response templates but there are also many that unfortunately do not (Airbnb being one of them). Where you are unable to use a templated response it's worth sending a separate message to the guest to articulate any other important details. However, be sure not to include the same details that the system has already sent the guest or you'll have them reaching for the delete button.

Standard Response

You are likely to have a generic response that you'll use 80% of the time when dealing with enquiries. Depending on the capability of the system you may not have to do much other than entering the price (and even then some systems will do this for you). Most of the major booking websites have templated responses that you can use.

When responding to a guest it's important to strike a balance in the amount of detail provided. The dreaded *Yes the property is available* one-line response is almost as frustrating for potential guests as those properties that overwhelm the guest with non-critical information. The worst example of this is when guests are bombarded with off-putting booking terms and conditions. Terms and conditions should be avoided in the initial enquiry response, but should be clearly viewable when the guest decides to book and pay. Here's an outline of the critical information you should provide:

- Guest name (otherwise it will appear cold and impersonal)
- Name of the property and location (town/suburb)
- Link to the property (must be the hyperlink of the website the booking came through or it will be blocked)

- Description of the property (including location)
- Requested dates and number of nights
- Total price (don't expect the guest to calculate the total price by adding up confusing fees!)
- Instructions on how to proceed with the booking
- Contact name (unfortunately email address, phone number and your website will be blocked).

As you get to know your audience better you can create specific template responses for your key target groups. For example, a cabin in the mountains may highlight walks for ramblers whilst a property by the sea might highlight water sports facilities.

An owner says ...

Whenever someone mentions that they are bringing the family dog we use a pet-friendly enquiry response template where we extol the pet-friendly features of our property.

Discount Response

It's also worthwhile setting up templates for any discounts or special deals that you currently use. This doesn't have to be hugely different to your generic response but you should make it clear within the text that they are getting a special deal. Don't just tell them the percentage discount or number of nights free – be specific about the amount they are saving as this is more impactful.

Declining Guests

There will always be situations where you don't want to accept particular guests. In these situations a polite decline response with a reason for the decline is all that is required. If you don't provide a reason for the decline guests may get upset. Whatever you do, don't upset or be rude to them – it's very easy for them to take it out on your property on social media. It's also possible that if you are courteous with these guests they may come back to you at a later date with a more suitable party.

If the guest has booked using Instant Booking and has clearly breached your rules, ask the guest to cancel the booking so that you are not penalised. If the guest refuses you can escalate this to the booking website and they will cancel the booking without penalty.

An owner says ...

We are always as polite as possible when declining guests. You never know who they might mention your property to if you treat them with respect. If our property is too small for the party we often refer other properties in the area. This is a good way to look after our own community of holiday rental owners and other owners often reciprocate.

Phone

Due to restrictions of the booking websites, guest or owner phone numbers are not made available until after the booking has been confirmed.

Some owners like to call the guests as a form of welcome and to identify any special requirements or answer any questions. This comes across as a bit invasive and a little creepy. Guests don't want to be reminded that they are staying at someone else's property, they want to feel like it's their home for a few days without the feeling that someone is looking over their shoulder big-brother style. A comprehensive Guest Guidebook should be all the information the guest needs prior to their stay.

Following Up

When you've sent a quote in response to a guest enquiry it's important to remember to follow up with them afterwards. This is an important step that many holiday rental owners forget. With busy lives and email overwhelm it's easy for your initial response to be lost in a sea of information and choices. Given that a guest may have submitted several enquiries, a follow-up message can help set your property apart in the guest's mind. It can also provide you with the opportunity to sell other features of your property that you didn't mention in the first response or to reinforce some of the property's key selling points.

Booking and Payment

Instant Bookings

All of the major websites offer Instant Booking functionality. What this means is that the guest can find a property and pay online to secure the booking, much like booking a hotel room via a traditional hotel website. The holiday rental owner then receives a confirmation of the booking.

As previously mentioned, guests are increasingly expecting a book-now hotel-style experience and holiday rental booking websites are starting to cater for this more and more. Holiday rentals offering this functionality stand a much better chance of receiving bookings as compared to those who do not. This is because the websites promote properties with Instant Booking ahead of those which don't have it.

What holiday rental owners need to be careful with is to ensure that their pricing is always up-to-date and correct. There's nothing more frustrating than to receive a booking then realise that you have under-priced the dates. The other thing that owners need to be careful with is the number and type of guests permitted. Whilst some websites will allow you to cancel a booking without penalty if the type of group breaches your terms and conditions (e.g. Airbnb), some websites do not allow this.

Many owners feel uncomfortable not having the final say as to whether they will accept a booking. The bottom line is that if you don't feel comfortable with Instant Booking functionality you don't have to provide the option to guests, but your bookings will suffer significantly as a result.

Guest Acceptance

If the guest decides that they want to book your property (and they aren't using Instant Booking functionality) they will reply to your enquiry via the booking website. At this point it's important to get payment from the guest to secure the booking as quickly as you can.

Don't make the mistake of reserving dates for the guest prior to payment being received. Make it clear to the guest that dates are not reserved until the deposit payment is received. This acts as an incentive for the guest to pay and finalise the booking as they may be worried that they may lose the booking. Do not give the guest longer than 24 hours to pay.

Payment Methods

Today, all payments must come through the booking website's payment system – the only exception being Booking.com. Booking.com has a payment system but it is limited in functionality. If you choose to, you are able to obtain the customer's credit card details from the system and process it yourself. However this will require you to use your own payment platform which can be complex to set up and costs additional fees. With Booking.com if you want to charge a bond you will have to do this manually via a separate payment system that you will need to set up.

Updating Calendars

When the guest pays and the booking is confirmed, it's important that your calendars are synchronised. This requires a one-off set-up of exporting/importing the iCal link from each booking website to the other. For example, export the HomeAway iCal link into Airbnb and Booking.com, export the Airbnb link to HomeAway and Booking.com, etc. This way all of your calendars will sync within a few minutes. There is a small window where a double booking could occur so if you are in a peak period with lots of bookings coming in, it doesn't hurt to log into each website and refresh the calendar to make sure the sync is up-to-date.

Sending Guests Information

A very important part of the guest experience relates to the information that you send the guest once their booking has been confirmed (Guest Guidebook).

Note: many systems will generate this information for the guest so you may not need to include all of this information. Adjust your guest information template to suit.

Here's what should be included:

- Confirmation of booking details:
- Dates
- Number of nights
- Total price
- Guest name
- Name of property
- Link to property
- Address

- Contact details
- Online Guest Guidebook (see earlier section)

Notifying Cleaners

You'll receive a confirmation email when the guest has paid which you can forward onto your cleaners to schedule in the clean when the guest leaves.

A guest check-out time of 11am and check-in time of 3pm gives your cleaning staff a 4-hour window (in the event of back-to-back bookings) which should be enough time to clean up to a three bedroom property. If you have a large property (e.g. four bedrooms or greater) you will need to have 2–3 cleaners cleaning the property simultaneously in order to decrease the amount of time required to complete the clean.

Cleaners should confirm that they have the clean booked in promptly, and it is good to set expectations around this. Normally 48 hours to confirm that the clean is scheduled in is reasonable. If you haven't received confirmation from the cleaners after 48 hours then follow up via email or text message. For urgent cleans (within 48 hours) it's a good idea to also text the cleaners or call them.

Once the clean has been confirmed by the cleaners you should add a note to your booking system for your records.

The Guest Stay

If you have a comprehensive Guest Guidebook in place and your property is well organised you might be surprised to know that you will not hear from the majority of your guests during their stay.

In our experience only about 5% of guests will contact us during their stay – sometimes to ask questions about how to operate facilities or to request late check-out, for example.

Some owners feel that they need to call or text the guest upon arrival as this provides a nice touch but this can make the guest feel like you are stalking them! Guests want to feel at home in your property and enjoy privacy, so it's important to strike a balance of making them feel at home without being overbearing.

An owner says ...

We make a point of not disturbing guests during their stay. Guests know that if they need us we are only a phone call or email away. By providing lots of information up front we eliminate the need for guests to contact us.

It's also a good idea to provide your immediate neighbours with your contact details so they can contact you should an issue arise. If you are vetting guests effectively then there should be limited problems with guest behaviour but it is always possible that one or two slip through the net. In these situations you can quickly end any unruly guest behaviour by calling the guest and reminding them of the terms and conditions that they have agreed to. It is always best to nip guest issues in the bud rather than turning a blind eye and letting neighbours suffer. Neighbours will be tolerant of holiday rentals if they are managed properly but can turn nasty and cause problems if issues frequently disturb them.

An owner says ...

If we receive a noise complaint we immediately contact the guest by phone. If the guests' behaviour does not improve after this warning we send our emergency contact to the property to speak to the guests in person.

Welcome Packs

Many holiday rental owners are now leaving welcome packs for guests. A welcome pack is usually a small gift basket of treats or goodies such as chocolates, biscuits or a bottle of wine. Whilst the welcome pack is becoming more common it isn't necessary if you are providing a well-equipped, clean property.

If you do want to provide a welcome pack it's important to factor in the cost of providing one each time, particularly if your cleaner or property manager has to put them together for guests. It's also important that your welcome pack contains unique items at an appropriate level of quality. There is little value to the guest in providing cheap snacks or cheesy souvenirs. Instead look to source locally made chocolates or a bottle of wine.

There is also an argument to say that you should not be spending money on welcome packs if your property isn't fully up to scratch. So if there are problems with the plumbing or the beds are lumpy, focus your money on getting the basics right before you even think about providing a welcome pack.

An owner says ...

We used to provide a lovely bottle of local wine as a welcome gift but we decided to stop after we realised that not a single guest had ever mentioned it. Having a great property that ticks every box is enough.

A guest says ...

We stayed at a holiday rental where the welcome pack consisted of a box of muesli bars and some bottled water. We would have rather they had provided nothing and instead fixed the wonky shower head in the bathroom.

Visitor Book

Having a visitor book at your property provides a nice touch. Guests like to read them to see who has visited your property from around the world and the (almost exclusively) kind comments help to reinforce the guest's own (hopefully positive) experience. Guests also enjoy leaving their mark in a little piece of history.

Guest Complaints

The majority of guest complaints can be resolved quickly but you (and your staff) must be on the ball! This means firstly that you are easy to contact. If you are a busy person stuck in meetings all day you need to provide additional contact details of someone who can get to your property in the blink of an eye!

As the majority of complaints involve issues of cleanliness or facilities not working as expected, it makes sense to have your cleaner as your emergency contact. If they have not cleaned something properly then by rights they should fix it. Therefore be sure to include their contact details within the Guest Guidebook. Be sure to let them know that you have done this and that there is the chance they may be called out at an unsociable hour.

The key to avoiding guest complaints is to keep your property in tiptop shape and to have all the facilities available as described in the property listing on websites.

However complaints do happen so here's how to handle the most common complaints:

- Cleaning issues: cleaner to attend property within 30 minutes to rectify issues

- Items missing: cleaner to help guests locate them or purchase new items

- Property damaged and in need of immediate repair: cleaner to contact owner to arrange maintenance staff to attend (or cleaner could contact staff directly)

- Appliance not working: cleaner to inform owner who will contact appliance repair staff to attend immediately.

In any of these situations having someone attend the property immediately can significantly help to diffuse any frustrations that the guest has. Most guests will appreciate a prompt response even if the problem cannot be resolved immediately.

In situations where you cannot rectify the problem immediately and the guest is inconvenienced you should offer the guest an appropriate refund as well as a credit for a future stay (so that they can have a more enjoyable experience next time). You should always apologise for the inconvenience even if it was outside of your control.

Emergencies and Disasters

Sometimes a guest will need to contact you regarding an urgent situation, however if your property is well maintained these moments will be rare. But it's important to be organised in advance so that if an issue occurs you can fix the problem quickly. You should have contact details of tradespeople on hand to cover the following potential issues:

- Handyman: general repairs and maintenance
- Plumber: toilet and shower problems, blocked drains
- Electrician: lighting, power outlets, power failures
- Appliance repairs: fridge, dishwasher, TV, washing machine, dryer

You should also have the contact details of retailer(s) from which you can quickly purchase an appliance in the event of a major failure. You must also have someone immediately available to pick up the appliance if you need to so that you don't have to rely on delivery by the retailer.

In the event that you are not contactable, ensure that you supply contact details of someone you trust in the local area (if you do not live near your property). This could be your cleaners or handyperson, for example.

Check-out

Be sure to include a checklist within your Guest Guidebook so that guests are clear on their check-out responsibilities. Generally you should ask guests to leave the property clean and tidy, although they shouldn't be expected to clean the property.

Some suggested check-out items you could include are:

- What to do with bedding/linen
- Switching off lights
- Closing windows and locking doors
- Putting dishes away
- Putting bins out for collection
- Cleaning BBQ or fireplace
- Cleaning up doggy dos or cigarette butts
- Putting the keys back (if lock box).

As well as adding to your Guest Guidebook you should display your checklist clearly at your holiday rental.

A guest says ...

Having clear instructions on what we need to do is helpful. Sometimes when holiday rentals charge a bond you are scared that they will take money out of your bond for not doing something properly when you leave. Instructions or a checklist make the process of checking out less stressful.

Cleaning and Inspection

Once the guest has checked out (hopefully at the designated time!) it's time for your cleaners to clean the property and to check for any issues. During the clean it's important that the cleaners follow any checklists to ensure that they are conducting a quality clean every time. As cleaners become familiar with the property they may stop using checklists, but it's important to try to be vigilant as to the quality of the clean.

As many owners do not live in close proximity to their holiday rentals you can encourage your guests to be your quality control team. You may wish to have a statement in your Guest Guidebook and also at your property stating:

'We aim for the highest standards of cleanliness and customer service. If anything isn't to your satisfaction or any items are missing (no matter how small) please contact us on <Mobile #> or <email address> as soon as you can after check-in.'

As an owner there are few things more frustrating than receiving a guest complaint *after* the guest has checked out. Encourage them to speak up so that you can rectify any issues immediately.

Stocking Up

It's also really important to ensure that your guests have access to all of the facilities advertised, including items that your cleaners will replenish at each clean, such as toilet paper, hand soap, dishwasher powder, cleaning cloths, etc. Whilst these things might seem trivial, imagine a guest arriving late at night after a long drive and finding no toilet paper at your property, or stacking the dishwasher only to find that they'll have to drive to the supermarket 15 minutes away to buy dishwasher tablets.

An owner says ...

We often found that when we stayed as guests in our own properties we would turn up to find the house beyond sparkling as the cleaners knew that we were staying! Now, to check on the quality of our cleaners we regularly create bookings under a pseudonym so that our cleaners do not know that we are checking in. This allows us to monitor the standard that guests receive rather than the standard that our cleaners provide us.

If you choose to provide late check-out, ensure that your cleaners clean and inspect the property within 48 hours of check-out as this is typically the period within which you can make deductions from the guest's bond via the system (e.g. Airbnb).

If any issues are found the cleaners should always take photos and supply these to you as evidence that you can show the guest.

It is a myth that guests will frequently cause damage to your property. The fact is that significant guest damage is rare.

One way to encourage good behaviour is by charging a bond for every stay. This encourages guests to look after the property.

Early Check-in/Late Check-out

Some guests will request an early check-in (or late check-out) and whilst this does increase the amount of work for the owner it's something that guests do appreciate. However, providing early check-in or late check-out on changeover days (when you have guests both arriving and departing) may put too much pressure on cleaning staff. You may wish to consider only providing variations to check-in/out times on non-changeover days.

There are always some guests that do not read the instructions or who will push their luck with regard to check-in/out time. Whilst this can be an inconvenience to cleaning staff it isn't worth upsetting the guest by charging extra fees or risking the possibility of a negative review.

An owner says ...

Guests don't always read the instructions. If guests arrive early we let them leave their bags at the property and suggest a local café or attraction that they can spend some time at until the house is ready.

Bond Refunds and Extra Charges

If your cleaners do report an issue it's critical to discuss with the guest before you attempt to withdraw any funds from their bond. Rather than accuse the guest of causing the problem try to take a non-confrontational approach to the issue. It has been known to happen that cleaners sometimes miss damage caused by previous guests and blame the guests that check-in after them.

Firstly, obtain photographic proof of the problem (without this there is little point in proceeding as you do not have any proof). Send the photos to the guest and politely ask them if they are aware of any damage being caused:

'Hi <Guestname>, our cleaners have notified us of some damage/a cleaning issue during their inspection today. I was just wondering if you could let me know what happened?'

The way in which this is worded is non-confrontational and does not blame the guest. It also gives them the opportunity to admit their guilt! In our experience if a guest has caused damage in some way they will usually admit to causing the damage and be more than willing to pay (however some will lie to avoid paying). If a guest is adamant that they did not cause any damage do not push the issue. It is better to absorb the cost of the damage (if not significant) than risk the possibility of a negative review.

In the unlikely event that you do have an issue with guests and need to withdraw funds from the guest's bond, the majority of online systems require you to submit a request within a 48-hour period of check-out. Some systems will gather information from both the guests and the owner (photos and receipts for broken items or extra cleaning charges) before going through an assessment (e.g. Airbnb). Others will simply allow you to withdraw funds along with a comment regarding the reason for the withdrawal.

As a holiday rental owner it's important to understand that little things will break and need to be replaced. Wine glasses, mugs, bowls and even the odd ornament will be broken over time. You should never attempt to claim these small breakages from the guest. Instead check what needs topped up on a quarterly basis or simply ask your cleaning staff to buy extras if they fall below a certain number; e.g. 12 wine glasses.

Guest Reviews

When you create a new listing it's important to remember that there is nothing wrong with your friends or family staying at the property. This way you can let them stay at a heavily discounted rate and in return they can leave you the crucial first reviews that will give guests confidence in your property. Just be sure that when you reduce the rate they jump on quickly to book it so that a guest doesn't book the discounted dates.

Once you do get some guest bookings and your guest has checked out and they are still basking in the warm and fuzzy glow of their break, it's time to hit them with a request for a review! As discussed previously, guest reviews are an important part of a potential guest's decision making process when booking a holiday rental. But most holiday rental owners make one crucial mistake when it comes to reviews; they wait for the guest to complete one. It's important that within 48 hours of check-out that you follow up with the guest asking them to leave a review (unless there is a chance they will not leave a positive review).

Some websites handle the review process better than others. Airbnb is a good example as they continually prompt the guest to leave a review, although there is nothing to say that you can't also message the guest asking for a review. When you do send the review request be sure to thank the guest for staying with you and stress how a review will help your business and your family (tug those heart strings!). You should include a hyperlink to your listing on the website that they booked through.

In the event that you receive an unexpectedly poor review or a comment that you find upsetting, it's important to try not to get emotional. In these situations it's important to speak to the guest over the phone if you can to understand why they have left a negative review or comment. Sometimes it can be as simple as a misunderstanding and in some cases a guest may choose to alter or remove a negative review.

An owner says ...

A guest mistakenly thought we had deducted a charge from their bond when in fact it was due to a system glitch. When we explained this to the guest they agreed to remove the negative review and instead posted a 5-star review!

Some of the main booking websites have the ability for holiday rental owners to review guests. The idea behind this was to help owners to avoid those (rare) troublesome guests but in effect it is very easy for a guest to set up a new profile and to start making bookings with a clean slate – the opposite is true for owners. In the event of a negative review it is a time-consuming process to set up the listing again, but it can be worth it if your review score is damaged significantly by a negative review.

Unfortunately guests have a huge amount of power when it comes to reviews. In a recent survey of owners, over 60% had been blackmailed by guests who said they'd leave a negative review if they didn't receive a part or whole refund on their booking.

An owner says ...

We had a guest turn up at a property and call up immediately saying that the place smelled of smoke, that bins were overflowing and that the advertised condiments were not available. He demanded a substantial refund. Upon sending round our staff to check they found there were no issues at all. Upon check-out we found that he had hidden the condiments behind the bin. Because we refused to refund him he left us a 1-star review which meant that we had to shut down the listing and set up a new one.

Marketing Your Property

Having good photos, great descriptions and being listed on the right websites is fundamental – but how effective are the other ways to market your property?

The following section will discuss a number of online and offline ways to market your property, and the effectiveness of each.

There has been a plethora of books written on each of these marketing mechanisms already so it isn't our intention to go into each of these in extensive detail. Where you wish to explore the topics further we recommend heading to the business section of your favourite bookshop to grab a book on the specific subject.

Building Your Guest Database

Building a guest database is a great way to avoid the fees charged by the booking websites. To maximise its effectiveness, you must have your own website with direct booking facility.

With most booking websites now blocking email addresses it is becoming harder and harder to build a database for direct marketing – but it isn't impossible. As each booking website provides access to the guest's phone number it is possible to bypass the booking website and ask for the guest's email via text or phone call. Be aware, however, that most guests will not be keen to share their email unless there is an advantage – so be sure to mention the savings they can achieve by booking direct.

A word of warning. In some countries there are large penalties for misusing customer email addresses without the correct level of consent – so please check your local laws as to what is required prior to adding a former guest to your email database, particularly if that address has originated from a booking website.

Blogging/Vlogging

If you have your own website, blogging can be a good way to attract visitors to your website. Search engines love new content so the more you create, the greater the chance of guests finding your website so long as you follow a few simple rules:

- Don't just blog about your property. You need to stand in the shoes of a guest and imagine what they would be searching for.
- Create content about the area; i.e. activities, great restaurants, hidden gems are a great starting point.
- Guests love Lists, such as the Top 5 Activities, Top 10 Restaurants, etc.

Blogging tends to be a long-term strategy and requires commitment. Writing and researching articles can be time consuming and not everyone is a wordsmith.

If you are a confident and clear talker you can always go down the path of recording video blogs (or vlogs for short). These can also be uploaded to your website and to help your website to be found on Google you can send them to a transcription firm then upload the text to your website. You can also upload your vlogs to YouTube and social media. Don't expect to have an army of followers overnight but if you stick with it you will gain extra exposure for your property. Keep your content short, interesting, professional and enjoyable.

Google My Business (https://business.google.com/)

Google offers a free service that lets you register your business (property) on the web so that it can be easily found.

With Google's presence on the Internet continually growing it's a great idea to set up a Google My Business account, so long as you make sure that you complete all of the information thoroughly. Missing contact details or poor quality photos can be instantly off-putting. When potential guests search for the name of your property on Google, the listing will appear prominently. This is of great advantage if guests are shopping around to compare prices. Having your listing easy to find means that they can quickly compare your prices with the booking websites to identify where the cheapest price is. Of course that should be your website.

Being on Google My Business means that your listing will also be published on Google maps which can be of great convenience to guests who may be navigating to the property on a mobile device or simply trying to find your contact details to ask a question.

Google AdWords

Google AdWords is a facility for you to advertise your property on Google. By signing up for an AdWords account and paying a fee (known as pay-per-click) your property can appear as an advert above the (free) search results.

Google AdWords is not a cost effective means of bringing in new enquiries. This is because when guests search for your property name you will be competing with the booking websites who have huge amounts of money to spend. This means that they are likely to outbid you every time. The second downside of this is that because the booking websites have so much money to spend it forces the cost per click up to uneconomical levels. In short you'll spend a lot of money and receive very few clicks unless you are prepared to invest significant amounts of time to increase your expertise.

Facebook

Facebook allows you the opportunity to list your property as a 'page' where you can add updates, photos, videos and details of your services. It is free to use but you will be prompted fairly regularly to boost the post via paid advertising or to create Facebook advertisements. You should avoid both.

Facebook, like blogging, can take considerable time (think years rather than months) to build up an audience where you can start to see results and you may find yourself spending inordinate amounts of time on it for very little return. Take a look at some of your local competitor's pages and you will typically see a sad state of early enthusiasm with a few posts and shares and very few updates. Even pages with hundreds of followers struggle to get one or two likes for a Facebook post. Given that you need around 200 views of your listing a day to receive an enquiry, Facebook simply takes too long to produce results.

Twitter, Instagram and Pinterest

Social media experts will tell you how great each of these are for your business, but for holiday rentals they are largely lame ducks. Requiring extensive effort for low returns they are best avoided unless you have a property with very unique features or aspect that is likely to go viral.

YouTube

With respect to generating traffic from YouTube itself, don't expect anything other than a few clicks a year. Where YouTube becomes valuable is when your property video is embedded into websites. Think of it as the icing on the cake of your property photos and description. Include your YouTube link on your website and other websites that allow it (government tourism websites, for example).

Awards

You may think that winning an award is beyond your humble property, but it's not. This is because very few holiday rental owners enter awards (despite there being dedicated categories for holiday rentals). Whilst the process for application can often be tediously detailed, if you can get through it there's a good chance you'll have something to show for it.

Despite being a humble beach shack, our property Hayes Beach House has won two major awards. This has given us additional credibility and exposure.

Newsletters

Of all the marketing methods mentioned so far, newsletters require the greatest effort. This is because they not only require a large database of guests to be effective but they require significant effort to not only create content of the newsletter (on a regular basis) but to also master the newsletter software. Whilst software such as Mailchimp is free, to create professional looking newsletter templates takes time and a reasonable understanding of technology. After all this effort the cut through of email marketing is low and the likelihood of a guest booking is even lower.

Print Advertising

Advertising an online listing in print is about as effective as a car without wheels. So no matter how many readers the magazine or newspaper says they have, or what special deals they have – give print advertising a huge body swerve.

eBay, Gumtree and Others

Almost as ineffective as print advertising but worse in that you'll have almost exclusively enquiries from deadbeats and time wasters who will try to negotiate $50 a night for your peak dates that you already booked months ago. Strictly for the lowest of budget properties.

Case Studies

This section details case studies of some properties managed by Professional Holiday Homes. They are two very different properties each with unique challenges, and we have turned them into incredibly successful properties.

Case Study 1: The Cottage* – Good things come in small packages

Fred and Mavis* own one of the South Coast's loveliest cottages. Beautifully appointed and a stone's throw to white sand and crystal clear waters, it is a little piece of paradise. But they had a major problem: no bookings.

Fred said, 'In our best year we did $18k in bookings. However we have never been able to repeat that success. We had listed on one website and the bookings had been consistent, but not spectacular.'

Then things changed. The bookings dropped off, and Fred and Mavis didn't know what to do to turn things around.

Mavis said, 'We contacted Professional Holiday Homes to see what they could do for us. Craig came out to assess the property …'

Craig: 'Sometimes when we view a property we quickly realise that the problem is with the property itself – this wasn't the case with the

163

cottage. The property was decorated and furnished to an exceptional standard. The problem was clearly in the setup of the listings online.

Firstly, the photos of the property were dark, fuzzy and unappealing, having been taken with a mobile phone. We sent in our amazing professional photographer who is a wizard at producing showcase images.

Pricing had been set at one price throughout the entire year with no separate fees for cleaning or linen. Owners often do that because it takes them less time. However, it has the effect that shorter stays are less profitable and peak periods are hugely under-priced meaning a missed opportunity.

We totally restructured their pricing so that shorter stays became as profitable as longer ones and we created thirteen different pricing seasons in order to maximise the income in the peak periods.

We also found that minimum stay periods were not correctly set which often meant that Fred and Mavis were receiving bookings that they then had to cancel. They didn't know that this penalised their property's ranking resulting in the property dropping down the search results, thus making it harder for guests to find. That flow-on effect catches owners unawares.

To combat this, minimum stay periods were set for long weekends and a minimum 2-night stay was set for other periods. This instantly eliminated the need to cancel bookings, stabilised the property, then improved the rank and the visibility to guests.

Being dependent on one booking website (HomeAway) was limiting the opportunities for bookings so we listed the property on Airbnb, Booking.com and a number of other websites in order to boost their opportunities for bookings.

In the 12-month period from when we took over management of the property we increased bookings to $64k. Not only were the owners financially much better off, but Fred and Mavis no longer had to deal with guest enquiries, processing bookings or handling guest questions. In short, more bookings and no stress!

*Names changed for privacy reasons

Case Study 2: The Rotunda – The 'Value' Beachfront

Rhonda and Ray had purchased their holiday home at Gerroa in 2001. The house was built in the late 1960s and still had some features of that time. They made a few cosmetic changes over the years and had some great family holidays and fabulous memories there.

Having an asset sitting empty for large parts of the year didn't make financial sense so in late 2018 they decided it was time to put the house on the holiday rental market. They did some further renovations such as painting, new furniture and of course added all the necessities such as new kitchen appliances, crockery, cutlery and linen. As a real estate agent herself, Rhonda decided to manage the property. She quickly realised that this was a big mistake …

Rhonda: 'It took up so much time – answering emails, taking bookings, logging on to all the websites, organising cleaning and repairs. It was all very tedious and was proving to be quite stressful!'

It was at this point that Rhonda contacted Professional Holiday Homes, having been referred to them by a friend.

After assessing the property we quickly set up the listings and took over management. We realised that the pricing was not optimised and set about creating different pricing seasons that were in tune with the market. We organised for professional photos to be taken, because the current photos did not show all of the rooms in the house.

We also provided a number of recommendations on how to improve the property including installing wifi and air conditioning. These improvements had an immediate impact.

Rhonda: 'Our bookings have skyrocketed since we gave the listing to Craig and the team at Professional Holiday Homes. The property requires very little action on our part. Professional Holiday Homes manage everything from the initial enquiry, right through to the guests actual stay and check out. As an owner, it's great as there isn't much to do on our end other than check that payments are correctly received into our account. This is how it should be!'

As a holiday home owner himself, Craig relates very well with us – he has been there and done that. His suggestions, advice and feedback on how to increase bookings offer value far above regular real estate agents. We are incredibly happy with the way things are going right now with an amazing result to date and many future bookings already in our calendar for the year ahead.

As a new listing with minimal bookings, the Rotunda has gone on to achieve $80k in bookings in its first year, with over $100k in bookings estimated for next year. The Rotunda is set to go from strength to strength.

About Professional Holiday Homes

We know what it's like setting up a new holiday rental and how important it is to get things right first time.

We have over a decade of award-winning experience managing holiday rentals. It's through this expertise that we know how to get you set up quickly and professionally so that you get bookings through the door quickly (and to keep them coming in).

We have no setup or ongoing fees – this includes professional photography and creating your online listings. Simply pay 15%+GST on the bookings you receive. Once your property is set up we manage the full end-to-end process including handling enquiries, bookings, guest questions, cleaning and more.

So if you'd like to find out how to have an incredibly professional holiday rental without the hassle, give us a call on (02) 91944411, email enquiries@professionalholidayhomes.com or visit us at www.professionalholidayhomes.com (even if you haven't bought a property yet).

Craig Reid, CEO and Founder – Professional Holiday Homes.

More Bookings, Happy Guests, No Stress

Acknowledgements

I'd like to thank the following people for their assistance with this book.

Our owners for trusting us to manage their properties. With every new property comes the opportunity to learn and improve. There's a little bit of every property we manage in this book.

Rhonda from The Rotunda and our other owners who very kindly allowed me to interview them for the case studies.

Tim Pye for taking the time out from writing some of Australia's best TV to review my book (I'm very humbled).

Jennifer Rhynehart & Geoff Carne for their unique owner-operator perspectives.

Vacation rental guru Matt Landau, for his glowing endorsement.

My mum, Helen, for proofreading yet another book.

My Editor and coach Robert, whose advice (as painful as it is to hear sometimes) made this a vastly better book!

Finally my biggest thanks go to my family ... my wife Romina and my children Oliver, Elliot, Sienna and Byron. Time is a precious thing, and while I was writing this book I missed spending that time with them. I hope they read this book one day and think it was worth it.

About the Author

Craig Reid is a multi award-winning holiday home owner and the CEO of Professional Holiday Homes.

Prior to starting Professional Holiday Homes Craig bought and ran two of the most successful holiday rentals in Australia. He also spent 20 years helping organisations improve their systems and processes.

He holds University qualifications in Marketing and Hospitality Management.

This is his fourth (and best) book.

Printed by Libri Plureos GmbH in Hamburg, Germany